Reading Comprehension
Nonfiction

Grade 1

Editorial Development: Barbara Allman
Lisa Vitarisi Mathews
Copy Editing: Anna Pelligra
Art Direction: Cheryl Puckett
Art and Photo Design: Kathy Kopp
Cover Design: Yuki Meyer
Illustration: Chris Vallo
Design/Production: Susan Lovell
Marcia Smith

EMC 3261
Visit
teaching-standards.com
to view a correlation
of this book.

**Correlated to
Current Standards**

**Congratulations on your purchase of some of the
finest teaching materials in the world.**

*Photocopying the pages in this book
is permitted for single-classroom use only.
Making photocopies for additional classes
or schools is prohibited.*

For information about other Evan-Moor products, call 1-800-777-4362,
fax 1-800-777-4332, or visit our website, www.evan-moor.com.
Entire contents © 2023 Evan-Moor Corporation
10 Harris Court, Suite C-3, Monterey, CA 93940-5773. Printed in USA.

Contents

What's in Every Unit?

The Guided Reading Level helps identify appropriate texts.

Student objectives and content-area concepts are indicated.

A suggested learning path helps you pace the lesson.

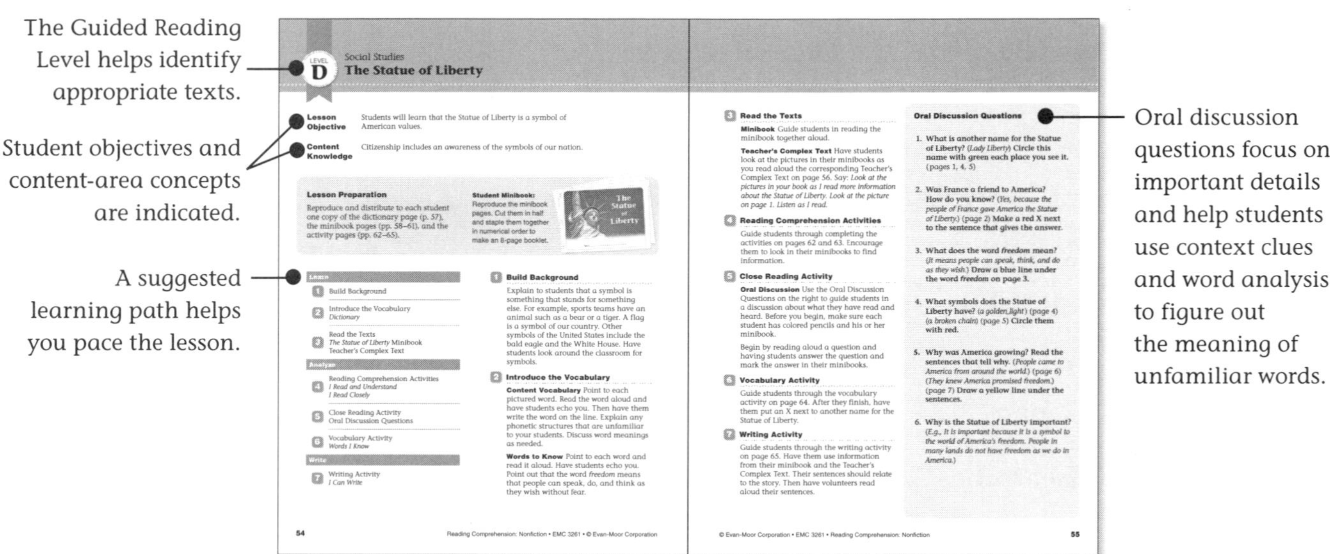

Oral discussion questions focus on important details and help students use context clues and word analysis to figure out the meaning of unfamiliar words.

Teacher's Complex Text includes:

• Complex ideas and content vocabulary

• Additional facts and details about the topic

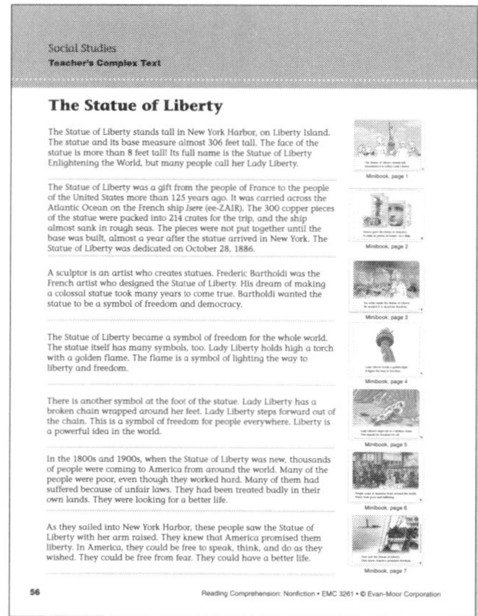

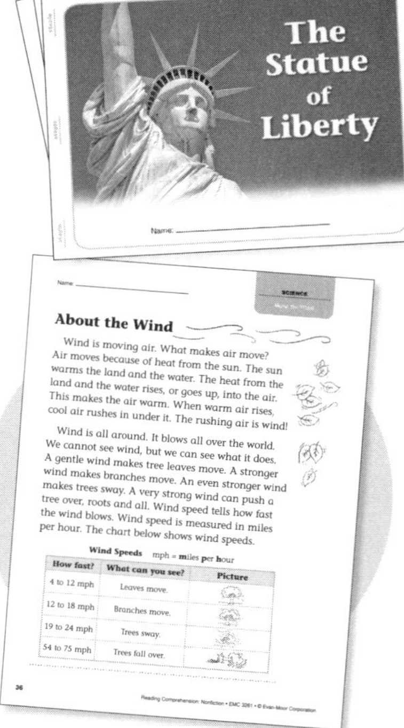

Reading Selections:

There are eight minibooks and two single-page reading selections.

Art and graphics provide additional information and context.

Controlled vocabulary and simplified concepts make the text accessible.

Student pages provide support for understanding content vocabulary and concepts.

Dictionary

A picture dictionary provides visual information for content vocabulary, helping students understand word meaning. The Words to Know lists additional vocabulary to introduce prior to reading the nonfiction text.

I Read and Understand

A reading comprehension activity asks students to answer questions about the nonfiction text, prompting them to examine it closely, and provides an informal assessment of students' understanding.

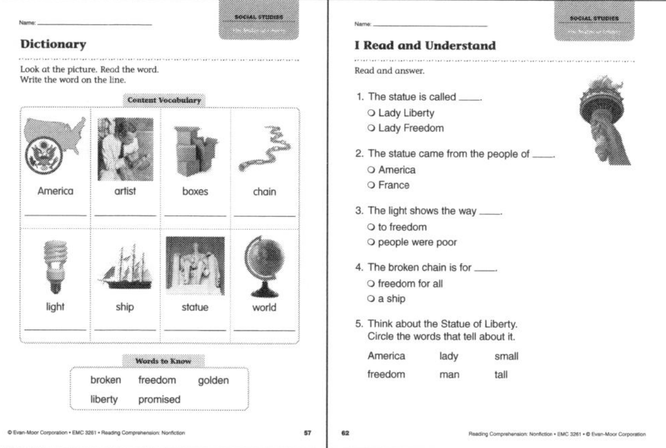

I Read Closely

A close reading activity presents students with pictures and sentences that ask students to connect text meaning and picture meaning.

Words I Know

A vocabulary activity provides students with another opportunity to interact with key words from the nonfiction text.

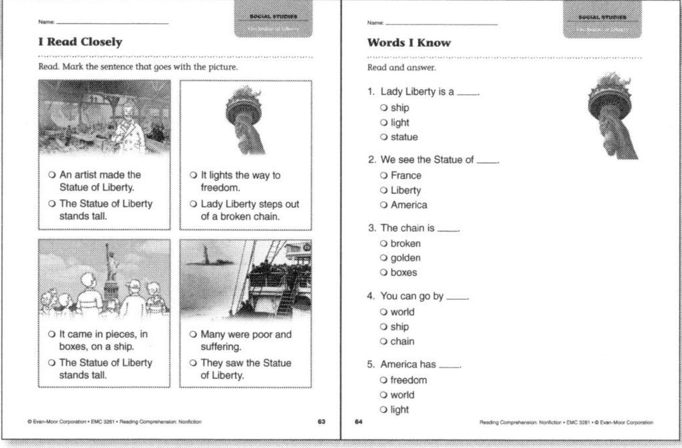

I Can Write

Units with minibooks culminate with a scaffolded writing assignment.

What I Learned

Units with two-page selections culminate with a text-based writing assignment.

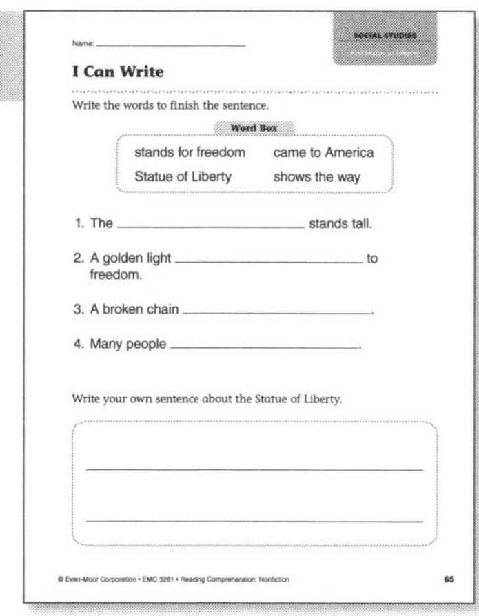
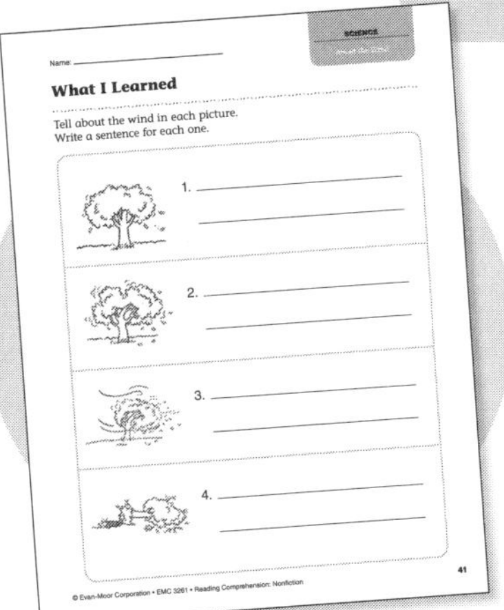

My Reading Journal

Name: _________________________________

Date _________________________________

I read about _________________________________

____

____

____

____

____

Date _________________________________

I read about _________________________________

____

____

____

____

____

How to Be a
Good Reader

Ask yourself these questions to help you understand what you read:

Main Idea and Details

What is the book mostly about?

What tells me more about the main idea?

Who and What

Who are the people in the book?

What animals are in the book?

What happens in the book?

Where and When

Where does the book take place?

When does the book take place?

Sequence

What happens first, next, and last?

What are the steps to do something?

Compare and Contrast

How are two people or things the same?

How are two people or things different?

Pictures

What do they show?

What do you learn from them?

Prediction

What clues does the book cover give?

What clues does the book title give?

What do I know already that will help?

Lesson Objective
Students will understand that living things need the sun's light and heat.

Content Knowledge
The sun is an energy source for living things.

Lesson Preparation

Reproduce and distribute to each student one copy of the dictionary page (p. 11), the minibook pages (pp. 12–15), and the activity pages (pp. 16–19).

Student Minibook: Reproduce the minibook pages. Cut them in half and staple them together in numerical order to make an 8-page booklet.

Learn

1 Build Background

2 Introduce the Vocabulary
Dictionary

3 Read the Texts
We Need the Sun Minibook
Teacher's Complex Text

Analyze

4 Reading Comprehension Activities
I Read and Understand
I Read Closely

5 Close Reading Activity
Oral Discussion Questions

6 Vocabulary Activity
Words I Know

Write

7 Writing Activity
I Can Write

1 Build Background

Explain to students that Earth is a planet. It takes Earth 365 days to travel around the sun; that is one year. The sun is an ordinary star, but to us it looks bigger and brighter than all the billions of other stars in space. That is because it is much closer to Earth. An object that is closer looks bigger.

2 Introduce the Vocabulary

Content Vocabulary Point to each pictured word. Read the word aloud and have students echo you. Then have them write the word on the line. Explain any phonetic structures that are unfamiliar to your students. Discuss word meanings as needed.

Words to Know Point to each word and read it aloud. Have students echo you. Point out that the word *live* can mean "to stay alive" or "to make a home in a place."

3 **Read the Texts**

Minibook Guide students in reading the minibook together aloud.

Teacher's Complex Text Have students look at the pictures in their minibooks as you read aloud the corresponding Teacher's Complex Text on page 10. Say: *Look at the pictures in your book as I read you more information about why we need the sun. Look at the picture on page 1. Listen as I read.*

4 **Reading Comprehension Activities**

Guide students through completing the activities on pages 16 and 17. Encourage them to look in their minibooks to find information.

5 **Close Reading Activity**

Oral Discussion Use the Oral Discussion Questions on the right to guide students in a discussion about what they have read and heard. Before you begin, make sure each student has colored pencils and his or her minibook.

Begin by reading aloud a question and having students answer the question and mark the answer in their minibooks.

6 **Vocabulary Activity**

Guide students through the vocabulary activity on page 18. After they finish, have them draw and color a sun and write the word *sun* below it.

7 **Writing Activity**

Guide students through the writing activity on page 19. Have them use information from their minibook and the Teacher's Complex Text. Their sentences should relate to the story. Then have volunteers read aloud their sentences.

Oral Discussion Questions

1. **What is the title of the book?** (*We Need the Sun*) **Draw an orange box around it.** (title page)

2. **The sun is important to people on Earth. What two things does the sun give us?** (*light, heat*) **Circle the words with red.** (page 2)

3. **Why is light important to us?** (*The light of the sun helps us see.*) **Draw a green line under the word that tells what the sun helps us do.** (*see*) (page 3)

4. **Why is heat important to us?** (*The heat of the sun keeps us warm.*) **Draw a blue line under the word that tells how the sun makes us feel.** (*warm*) (page 4)

5. **How does the light of the sun help plants?** (*It helps them grow.*) **Color the sun on this page yellow.** (page 5)

6. **How do plants help animals?** (*They are food for animals.*) **Read aloud the sentence that tells you this.** (*Animals eat plants for food.*) **Draw a green line under the sentence.** (page 6)

7. **In order to have food, people need the sun. Why?** (*The sun helps plants grow. Animals eat the plants. People eat food from the plants and animals.*) **Color the people and the sun on page 7.**

We Need the Sun

The sun is a star. We think of stars twinkling at night in the dark sky. Those stars are very far away from Earth. The sun is a star, too, but it is much closer to Earth. When we see the sun shining during the day, it is so bright that we cannot see the other stars. The sun is our day star. It is a very important star to Earth.

Minibook, page 1

The sun gives us light and heat. The sun is a ball of hot gases. It makes energy inside, at its center. The energy moves out into space. We see the sun's energy as light. We feel the sun's energy as heat. On hot days, we protect our bodies from the sun's energy. We cover up with clothes or sunscreen. We wear sun hats.

Minibook, page 2

The light of the sun helps us see. Our eyes see best in the light. The sun is always shining, but at night we do not see its light. Because Earth turns, at night we are turned away from the sun. If the sun did not shine, the whole earth would be dark. There would be no day.

Minibook, page 3

The heat of the sun keeps us warm. We can feel the heat of the sun when we are outdoors. We can feel the heat of the sun when we are inside a car. If the sun did not shine, the whole earth would always be cold.

Minibook, page 4

The light of the sun helps plants grow. The sun is important to green plants. Plants use the sun's energy. They use air, water, and sunlight to make their own food. Plants cannot live without the sun.

Minibook, page 5

Animals eat plants for food. Cows eat grass, which is a plant. Monkeys eat the fruit of plants. Birds eat the seeds of plants. People eat grains, fruits, vegetables, nuts, and seeds, too. Living things need plants for their food.

Minibook, page 6

People eat plants for food. People eat meat, eggs, and milk that come from animals, too. Without plants and animals, people would not have food. Living things on Earth need the sun in order to live.

Minibook, page 7

Name: _______________________

Dictionary

Look at the picture. Read the word.
Write the word on the line.

Content Vocabulary

animals

____

food

____

grow

____

light

____

people

____

plants

____

star

____

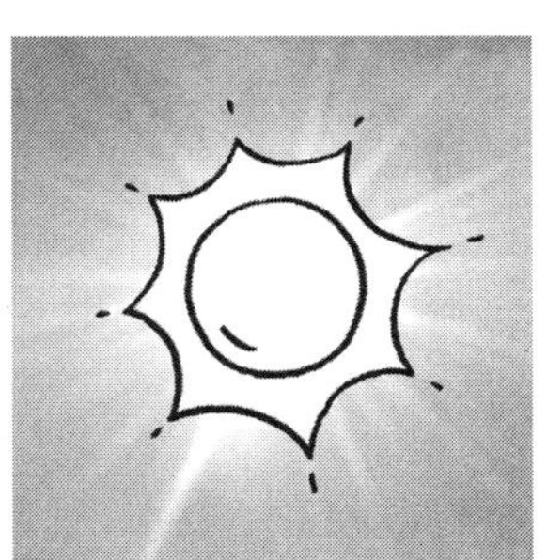

sun

____

Words to Know

heat	keeps	live
need	night	warm

We Need the Sun

Name: _______________

The sun is a star.

1

The sun gives us light and heat.

2

The light of the sun helps us see.

3

The heat of the sun keeps us warm.

4

The light of the sun helps plants grow.

5

Animals eat plants for food.

6

People eat plants. People eat food from animals. We need the sun to live.

7

I Read and Understand

Read and answer.

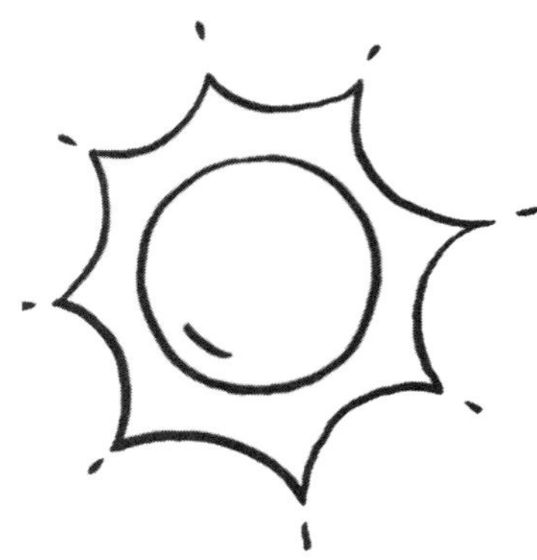

1. The sun is a ____.
   - O moon
   - O star

2. The sun gives us light and ____.
   - O heat
   - O earth

3. The sun helps plants ____.
   - O give
   - O grow

4. Plants are ____ for animals.
   - O food
   - O light

5. We need the ____ to live.
   - O people
   - O sun

Name: ___________________

I Read Closely

Read. Mark the sentence that goes with the picture.

○ The sun is a night star.

○ The light of the sun helps us see.

○ Animals eat plants for food.

○ The heat of the sun keeps us warm.

○ Plants and animals need food.

○ The sun gives us light and heat.

○ We need the sun to live.

○ The sun helps plants grow.

Words I Know

Read and answer.

1. Our sun is a _____.
   - ○ food
   - ○ people
   - ○ star

2. _____ are food.
   - ○ Star
   - ○ Plants
   - ○ Keeps

3. We _____ on Earth.
   - ○ warm
   - ○ night
   - ○ live

4. _____ eat plants.
   - ○ Plants
   - ○ Animals
   - ○ Need

5. Heat keeps us _____.
   - ○ warm
   - ○ light
   - ○ people

I Can Write

Write the words to finish the sentence.

Word Box

need the sun	a day star
and heat	plants grow

1. The sun is __________________.

2. The sun gives us light __________________.

3. The sun helps __________________.

4. People __________________.

Write a sentence. Tell one thing the sun gives us.

Little Blue Butterfly

LEVEL D

Lesson Objective Students will understand that living things need favorable habitats in order to survive.

Content Knowledge In order to survive, animals must find their own food, water, and shelter.

Lesson Preparation

Reproduce and distribute to each student one copy of the dictionary page (p. 23), the minibook pages (pp. 24–27), and the activity pages (pp. 28–31).

Student Minibook: Reproduce the minibook pages. Cut them in half and staple them together in numerical order to make an 8-page booklet.

Learn

1 Build Background

2 Introduce the Vocabulary
Dictionary

3 Read the Texts
Little Blue Butterfly Minibook
Teacher's Complex Text

Analyze

4 Reading Comprehension Activities
I Read and Understand
I Read Closely

5 Close Reading Activity
Oral Discussion Questions

6 Vocabulary Activity
Words I Know

Write

7 Writing Activity
I Can Write

1 Build Background

Explain to students that a habitat is the natural home of a plant or animal. All living things need a friendly habitat in order to live. But sometimes a habitat changes because nature changes. New buildings may use up land where plants and animals live. This puts plants and animals in danger. So people do things to help the plants and animals.

2 Introduce the Vocabulary

Content Vocabulary Point to each pictured word. Read the word aloud and have students echo you. Then have them write the word on the line. Explain any phonetic structures that are unfamiliar to your students. Discuss word meanings as needed.

Words to Know Point to each word and read it aloud. Have students echo you. Point out that the word *save* can mean "to keep something from danger" or "to keep from spending money."

3 **Read the Texts**

Minibook Guide students in reading the minibook together aloud.

Teacher's Complex Text Have students look at the pictures in their minibooks as you read aloud the corresponding Teacher's Complex Text on page 22. Say: *Look at the pictures in your book as I read you more information about the little blue butterfly. Look at the picture on page 1. Listen as I read.*

4 **Reading Comprehension Activities**

Guide students through completing the activities on pages 28 and 29. Encourage them to look in their minibooks to find information.

5 **Close Reading Activity**

Oral Discussion Use the Oral Discussion Questions on the right to guide students in a discussion about what they have read and heard. Before you begin, make sure each student has colored pencils and his or her minibook.

Begin by reading aloud a question and having students answer the question and mark the answer in their minibooks.

6 **Vocabulary Activity**

Guide students through the vocabulary activity on page 30. After they finish, ask them to find the word *butterfly* three times on the page and circle it with blue.

7 **Writing Activity**

Guide students through the writing activity on page 31. Have them use information from their minibook and the Teacher's Complex Text. Their sentences should relate to the story. Then have volunteers read aloud their sentences.

Oral Discussion Questions

1. **What is the title of the book?** (*Little Blue Butterfly*) **Draw a blue line over the title.** (title page)

2. **What animal is named in the title?** (*butterfly*) **Color the butterfly blue.** (title page)

3. **Why is the plant important to the butterfly?** (*The plant is a habitat. A butterfly lives there.*) **Make a red X next to the sentence that tells you.** (page 1)

4. **A butterfly grows in stages. It starts as an egg. A caterpillar hatches from the egg. What does the caterpillar eat?** (*the flower*) **Circle the word with green.** (page 2)

5. **In the next stage, the caterpillar turns into a pupa. What does the pupa do?** (*goes to sleep under the plant*) **Draw an orange line under the words that tell you.** (page 3)

6. **Next, the pupa turns into a butterfly. Make a purple X on the page that tells what the butterfly does.** (*The little blue butterfly drinks from the flower.*) (page 4)

7. **Where does the butterfly's plant grow?** (*by a big airport and by a factory*) **Draw a red line under the words *airport* and *factory*.** (page 5)

8. **How do people help save the butterfly?** (*They grow more plants.*) **Circle the word *save*. Color the people.** (page 6)

Little Blue Butterfly

The El Segundo Blue Butterfly spends its whole life with only one type of plant. It is called the seacliff buckwheat plant. This plant is the El Segundo Blue Butterfly's habitat. The tiny butterfly can only live near this plant.

Minibook, page 1

Every year in late summer, the eggs of the El Segundo Blue Butterfly hatch into caterpillars. The caterpillar eats the seeds in the seacliff buckwheat's flowers. It is the only food the caterpillar eats.

Minibook, page 2

After eating buckwheat flowers for about a month, the caterpillar enters another stage as a pupa (chrysalis). By September, the pupas are asleep at the foot of the buckwheat plant, among the dead leaves. They sleep there all winter long.

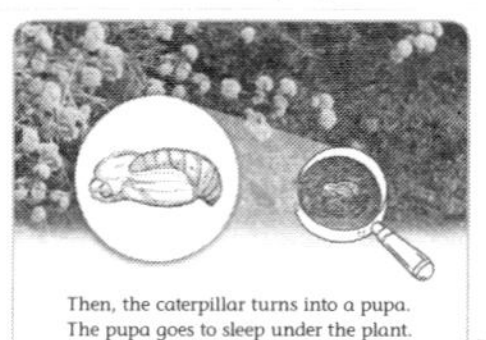

Minibook, page 3

By the next summer, the buckwheat flowers bloom again. The pupas have changed into tiny adult butterflies less than one inch across. Some are about the size of a thumbnail. The wings of the butterfly are blue on top, and gray underneath. Its wings have dark spots, with orange coloring on the back wings. The butterfly lives for only a few days. It drinks nectar from the flowers of the buckwheat plant and lays its eggs on the plant.

Minibook, page 4

As you can see, the seacliff buckwheat plant is very important to the tiny El Segundo Blue Butterfly. The buckwheat plant grows in only a few places. One place is the sand dunes on land owned by Los Angeles International Airport. Another place is on land owned by Standard Oil, where there is a factory called an oil refinery.

Minibook, page 5

In the 1970s, people discovered that there were fewer and fewer El Segundo Blue Butterflies every year. In 1976, fewer than 500 butterflies were counted. The airport and factory buildings had taken away some of the land good for growing buckwheat plants. People decided to help save the butterflies by growing more buckwheat plants and protecting the plants that were already growing.

Minibook, page 6

Today, people watch over the plants and butterflies. People from the airport and the oil refinery help them. They grow more buckwheat plants as habitat for the butterflies. They remove the weeds and other plants that creep in. Now, there are 60,000 to 70,000 butterflies each year. The story of the El Segundo Blue Butterfly is the story of people caring for nature's tiny creatures.

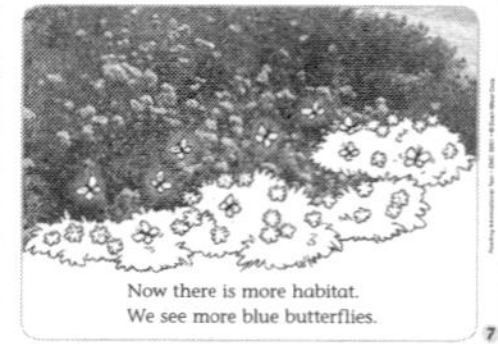

Minibook, page 7

Name: ______________________________

Dictionary

Look at the picture. Read the word.
Write the word on the line.

Content Vocabulary

airport

____

butterfly

____

caterpillar

____

factory

____

habitat

____

plant

____

pupa

____

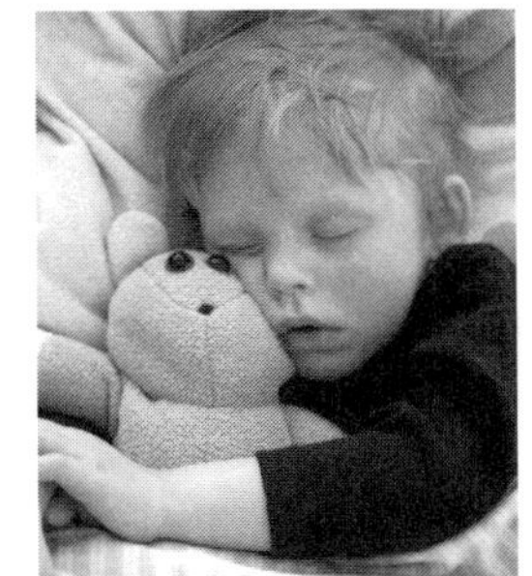

sleep

____

Words to Know

blue	butterflies	drinks	eats
grow	more	save	under

Little Blue Butterfly

Name: ___________________________

These plants are a habitat for butterflies.
Butterflies begin as caterpillars.

1

First, the caterpillar eats the flower.

2

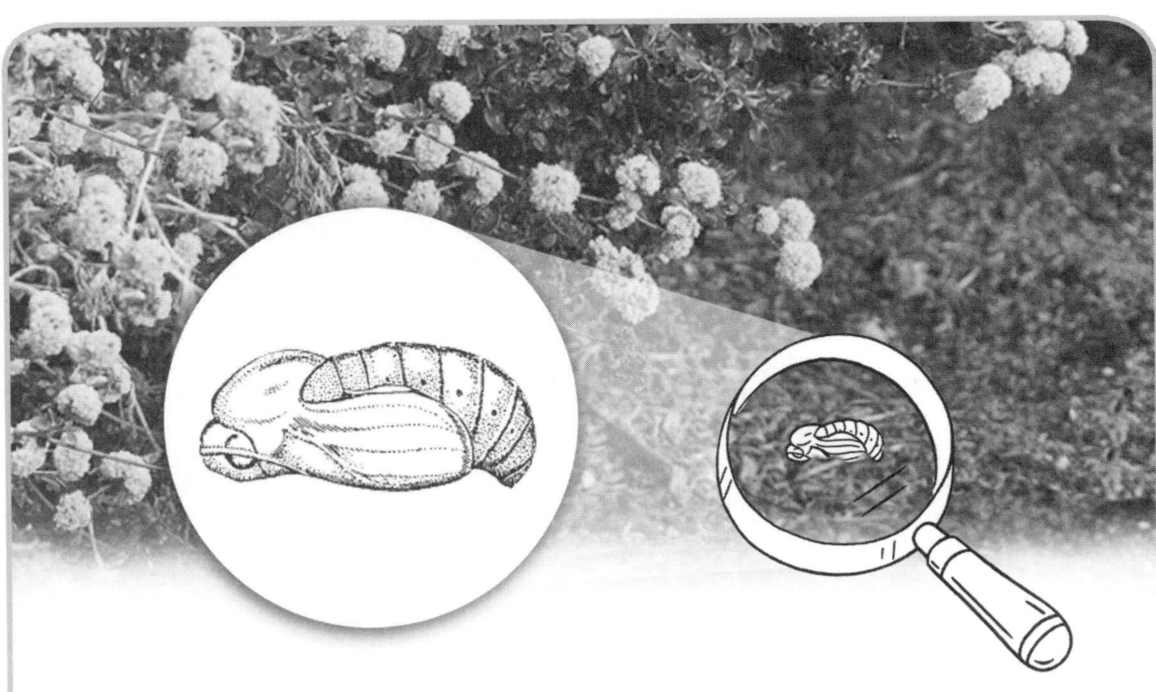

Then, the caterpillar turns into a pupa.
The pupa goes to sleep under the plant.

3

The pupa turns into a butterfly.
The little blue butterfly drinks from the flower.

4

The plant grows by a big airport. It grows by
a factory, too. This is not good for the butterfly.

5

People want to save the butterfly.
So they grow more plants.

6

Now there is more habitat.
We see more blue butterflies.

7

Reading Comprehension: Nonfiction • EMC 3261 • © Evan-Moor Corporation

I Read and Understand

Read and answer.

1. A _____ can be a habitat.
   - ○ butterfly
   - ○ plant

2. The caterpillar eats the _____.
   - ○ flower
   - ○ butterfly

3. People _____ the blue butterfly.
   - ○ drink
   - ○ save

4. People _____ more plants.
   - ○ grow
   - ○ sleep

5. Now we see more _____ butterflies.
   - ○ big
   - ○ blue

Name: _______________________________

I Read Closely

Read. Mark the sentence that goes with the picture.

○ The caterpillar eats
the flower.

○ The pupa goes to
sleep under the plant.

○ Now there is more
habitat.

○ The plant grows by
a big airport.

○ The little blue butterfly
drinks from the flower.

○ People want to save
the butterfly.

○ We see more blue
butterflies.

○ It grows by a factory,
too.

Words I Know

Read and answer.

1. A ____ drinks.
   - ○ pupa
   - ○ butterfly
   - ○ factory

2. Plants ____ there.
   - ○ grow
   - ○ sleep
   - ○ save

3. The butterfly is ____.
   - ○ more
   - ○ many
   - ○ blue

4. A ____ eats.
   - ○ caterpillar
   - ○ habitat
   - ○ factory

5. The plant is a ____.
   - ○ butterfly
   - ○ habitat
   - ○ airport

Name: ___________________________

I Can Write

Write the words to finish the sentence.

Word Box

more blue butterflies	eat and grow
little blue butterfly	be a habitat

1. A plant can ___________________________.

2. A butterfly can ___________________________.

3. People can save the ___________________________.

4. You can see ___________________________.

Write a sentence about the butterfly.

____

____

Lesson Objective Students will understand that wind is moving air and that we can observe what it does.

Content Knowledge Weather can be described and measured by temperature, wind speed, and direction.

Lesson Preparation

Reproduce and distribute to each student one copy of the dictionary page (p. 35), the student text (p. 36), and the activity pages (pp. 37–41).

Learn

1 Build Background

2 Introduce the Vocabulary
Dictionary

3 Read the Texts
About the Wind Student Text
Teacher's Complex Text

Analyze

4 Reading Comprehension Activities
I Read and Understand
I Read Closely

5 Close Reading Activity
Oral Discussion Questions

6 Vocabulary Activity
Words I Know

Write

7 Writing Activities
I Can Write
What I Learned

1 Build Background

Explain to students that air is all around us, though we cannot see it. Air can be warm or cold. Air is made up of tiny particles called molecules. Molecules are so tiny we can't see them. In cold air, the molecules are close together. This makes cold air heavier, and it moves down. Warm air molecules are farther apart.

2 Introduce the Vocabulary

Content Vocabulary Point to each pictured word. Read the word aloud and have students echo you. Then have them write the word on the line. Explain any phonetic structures that are unfamiliar to your students. Discuss word meanings as needed.

Words to Know Point to each word and read it aloud. Have students echo you. Point out that the word *rise* can mean "to go up" or "to stand up."

3 Read the Texts

Student Text Guide students in reading the text together aloud.

Teacher's Complex Text Have students look at the chart in their text and listen as you read aloud the corresponding Teacher's Complex Text on page 34. Say: *Look at the pictures and chart as I read you more information about how wind is made and how it is measured. Listen as I read.*

4 Reading Comprehension Activities

Guide students through completing the activities on pages 37 and 38. Encourage them to look in their text to find information.

5 Close Reading Activity

Oral Discussion Use the Oral Discussion Questions on the right to guide students in a discussion about what they have read and heard. Before you begin, make sure each student has colored pencils and his or her text.

Begin by reading aloud a question and having students answer the question and mark the answer in their text.

6 Vocabulary Activity

Guide students through the vocabulary activity on page 39. After they finish, have them circle the two sets of word opposites: *warm* and *cool* / *strong* and *gentle.*

7 Writing Activities

Guide students through the *I Can Write* activity. Have them use information from their text and the Teacher's Complex Text. Their sentences should relate to the story. For the *What I Learned* activity, have them use information from their text to write sentences about wind.

Oral Discussion Questions

1. What is the title of the text? (*About the Wind*) Draw a blue line under it.

2. Look at the first paragraph of the text. What question does it answer? (*What makes air move?*) Draw a green line under the question.

3. The first paragraph explains step by step how wind happens. First, the sun warms two things. What are they? (*land, water*) Draw a red circle around each one.

4. Draw a brown line under the first sentence and the last sentence in paragraph 1. What do they both tell us? (*They both tell us what wind is.*)

5. Look at the second paragraph of the text. It tells a way to use our eyes to find out about wind speed. How can we do that? (*by looking at how much the trees are moving when the wind blows*)

6. Look at the Wind Speeds chart. What do the letters *mph* stand for? (*miles per hour*) Make an X by the answer.

7. How fast is the wind blowing when tree branches move? (*12 to 18 mph*) Draw a purple line under the answer in the chart.

8. What do the trees do when wind speeds are 19 to 24 miles per hour? (*Trees sway.*) Draw an orange line under the answer in the chart.

About the Wind

What is wind? Wind is moving air. It is the same air that everyone breathes. What makes air move? It begins with the sun's energy. The sun sends light and heat energy to Earth. This warms the land and the water. Then heat from the land and water is reflected back into the air. This heat warms the air. Because warm air molecules are farther apart, warm air is lighter. The warm air rises. Cool air is heavier. It rushes in under the warm air and takes its place. We call the rushing air wind.

Just as air is everywhere, wind is all around us, too. It blows all over the world. We cannot see wind, but we can see what it does. Wind can blow through your hair or toss your hat. Wind can make a kite fly high or make a flag stand out. A gentle wind makes tree leaves rustle. A stronger wind makes branches shake. An even stronger wind makes trees sway back and forth. A very strong wind can push a tree right over, pulling its roots up out of the ground. Wind speed is a measure of how fast the wind blows. Wind speed is measured in miles per hour, just as a car's speed is measured. The chart below shows how a tree looks at different wind speeds. The letters *mph* in the chart stand for *miles per hour*.

Wind Speeds

mph = **m**iles **p**er **h**our

How fast?	What can you see?	Picture
4 to 12 mph	Leaves move.	
12 to 18 mph	Branches move.	
19 to 24 mph	Trees sway.	
54 to 75 mph	Trees fall over.	

Name: _______________________________

Dictionary

Look at the picture. Read the word.
Write the word on the line.

Content Vocabulary

air

____

branches

____

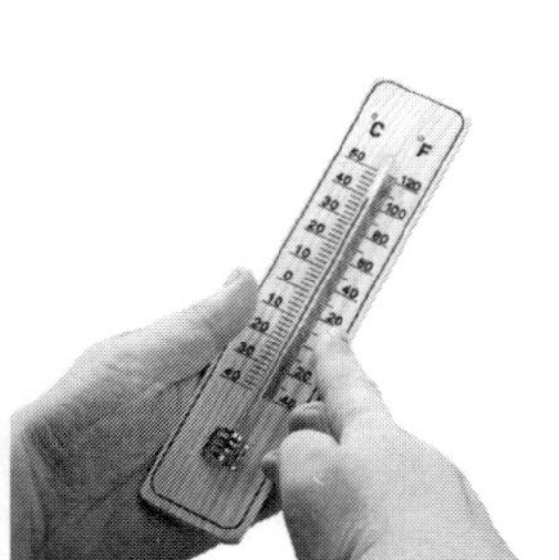

heat

____

land

____

leaves

____

roots

____

water

____

wind

____

Words to Know

cool	gentle	rises
stronger	sway	warm

About the Wind

Wind is moving air. What makes air move? Air moves because of heat from the sun. The sun warms the land and the water. The heat from the land and the water rises, or goes up, into the air. This makes the air warm. When warm air rises, cool air rushes in under it. The rushing air is wind!

Wind is all around. It blows all over the world. We cannot see wind, but we can see what it does. A gentle wind makes tree leaves move. A stronger wind makes branches move. An even stronger wind makes trees sway. A very strong wind can push a tree over, roots and all. Wind speed tells how fast the wind blows. Wind speed is measured in miles per hour. The chart below shows wind speeds.

Wind Speeds   mph = **m**iles **pe**r **h**our

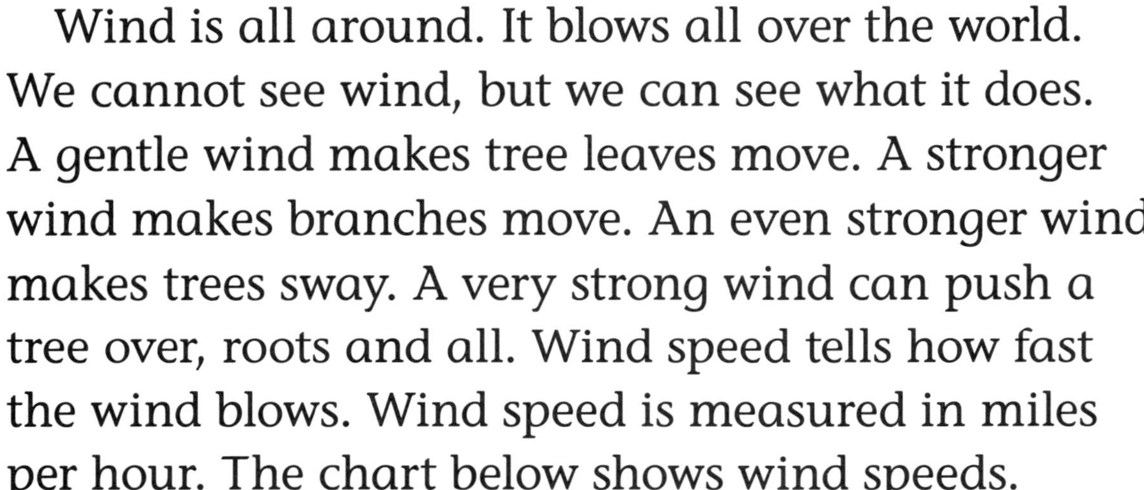

How fast?	What can you see?	Picture
4 to 12 mph	Leaves move.	
12 to 18 mph	Branches move.	
19 to 24 mph	Trees sway.	
54 to 75 mph	Trees fall over.	

Name: ___________________________

I Read and Understand

Read and answer.

1. Wind is moving ____.

   ○ heat

   ○ air

2. When warm air rises, cool air ____.

   ○ rushes in

   ○ also rises

3. We can see ____.

   ○ the wind

   ○ what wind does

4. Leaves move in ____.

   ○ a gentle wind

   ○ no wind

5. A tree can fall if the wind is ____.

   ○ 12 mph

   ○ 54 mph

Name: _______________________

I Read Closely

Read the question. Look at the picture. Write your answer.

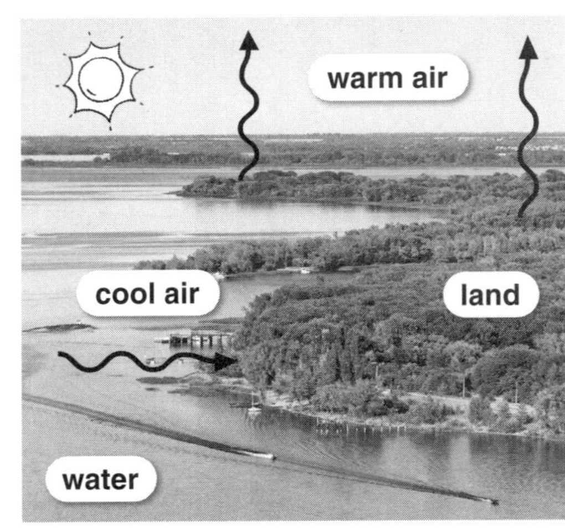

1. What happens when warm air rises?

____

____

2. Can we see the wind?

____

____

3. How fast is the wind if only tree leaves move?

____

____

Name: _______________________

Words I Know

Read and answer.

1. _____ from the fire kept us warm.
   - ○ Air
   - ○ Heat
   - ○ Water

2. We all _____ from our seats.
   - ○ rise
   - ○ strong
   - ○ land

3. The weather is _____.
   - ○ land
   - ○ water
   - ○ cool

4. The plant has _____ under the ground.
   - ○ branches
   - ○ roots
   - ○ leaves

5. A _____ wind took my hat!
   - ○ strong
   - ○ gentle
   - ○ sway

I Can Write

Write the words to finish the sentence.

Word Box

the warm air	push a tree over
the wind blows	and the water

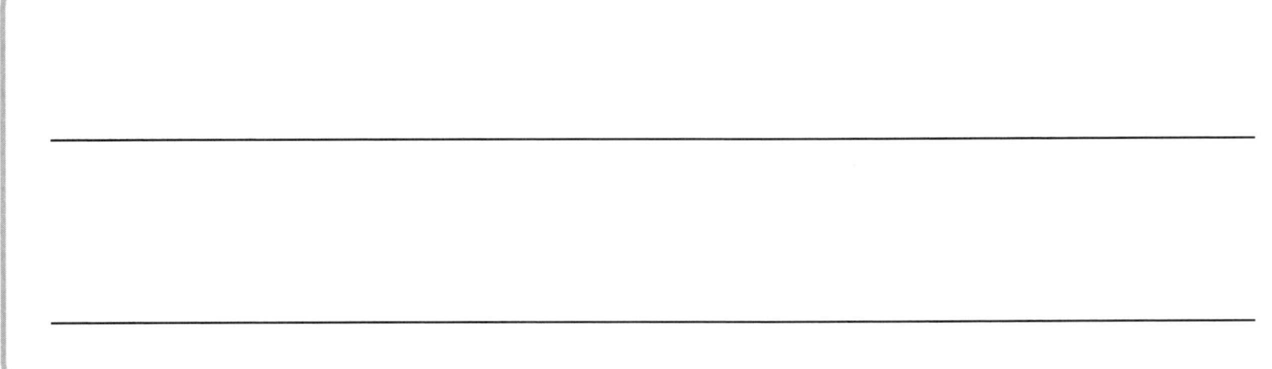

1. Heat from the sun warms the land

   _________________________.

2. Cool air rushes in under ___________________________.

3. A very strong wind can ___________________________.

4. Wind speed tells how fast ___________________________.

Write a sentence. Tell one fact about wind.

____

____

Name: _______________________________

What I Learned

Tell about the wind in each picture.
Write a sentence for each one.

1. _______________________________

____

2. _______________________________

____

3. _______________________________

____

4. _______________________________

____

Lesson Objective Students will learn that water has three different forms (states): solid, liquid, and gas.

Content Knowledge Water is matter that can change into solid, liquid, and gas.

Lesson Preparation

Reproduce and distribute to each student one copy of the dictionary page (p. 45), the minibook pages (pp. 46–49), and the activity pages (pp. 50–53).

Student Minibook: Reproduce the minibook pages. Cut them in half and staple them together in numerical order to make an 8-page booklet.

Learn

1 Build Background

2 Introduce the Vocabulary
Dictionary

3 Read the Texts
Water Minibook
Teacher's Complex Text

Analyze

4 Reading Comprehension Activities
I Read and Understand
I Read Closely

5 Close Reading Activity
Oral Discussion Questions

6 Vocabulary Activity
Words I Know

Write

7 Writing Activity
I Can Write

1 Build Background

Explain to students that a space traveler looking down at Earth sees a blue planet. Earth looks blue because most of it is covered by water. Oceans, rivers, streams, snowy mountain peaks, and clouds are places that hold water. Water is very important—living things need water to survive. The water on Earth moves and changes.

2 Introduce the Vocabulary

Content Vocabulary Point to each pictured word. Read the word aloud and have students echo you. Then have them write the word on the line. Explain any phonetic structures that are unfamiliar to your students. Discuss word meanings as needed.

Words to Know Point to each word and read it aloud. Have students echo you. Point out that the word *cold* can refer to the temperature of something or an illness.

3 **Read the Texts**

Minibook Guide students in reading the minibook together aloud.

Teacher's Complex Text Have students look at the pictures in their minibooks as you read aloud the corresponding Teacher's Complex Text on page 44. Say: *Look at the pictures in your book as I read you more information about water. Look at the picture on page 1. Listen as I read.*

4 **Reading Comprehension Activities**

Guide students through completing the activities on pages 50 and 51. Encourage them to look in their minibooks to find information.

5 **Close Reading Activity**

Oral Discussion Use the Oral Discussion Questions on the right to guide students in a discussion about what they have read and heard. Before you begin, make sure each student has colored pencils and his or her minibook.

Begin by reading aloud a question and having students answer the question and mark the answer in their minibooks.

6 **Vocabulary Activity**

Guide students through the vocabulary activity on page 52. After they finish, have them find the word *water* three times on the page and circle it with blue.

7 **Writing Activity**

Guide students through the writing activity on page 53. Have them use information from their minibook and the Teacher's Complex Text. Their sentences should relate to the story. Then have volunteers read aloud their sentences.

Oral Discussion Questions

1. **What is the title of the book?** (*Water*) **Color the title blue.** (title page)

2. **What does the title tell you about the book?** (*It has information about water.*)

3. **Water has different forms (states). Name the three forms of water.** (*1. liquid—faucet picture, 2. solid—ice cube picture, 3. gas—teakettle picture*) **Write the numbers 1, 2, and 3 above their pictures on page 1.**

4. **How is rain made?** (*Clouds are made of tiny drops of water. If the drops get big enough, they fall as rain.*) **Draw a purple line under the sentence that tells what happens if the drops get big enough.** (page 2)

5. **Name two kinds of solid water.** (*snow, ice*) **Circle the words with red.** (page 3)

6. **What happens when snow and ice melt?** (*They become liquid water. Snow and ice melt into liquid water.*) **Draw a yellow line under the sentence that helped you answer the question.** (page 4)

7. **Though you can't see it, where is water vapor?** (*in the air*) **In the picture on page 5, what is evaporating?** (*puddles*) **Mark them with an X.**

8. **What do you have inside your body that is watery?** (*blood*) **In the picture on page 6, what is the girl eating?** (*a juicy orange*) **Color it orange.**

9. **Where did you see water today? Was it being used for something?** (*E.g., The sprinklers were on at school. The water helps the grass grow.*)

Water

Water makes life on Earth possible. Water can be found in many places and in different forms. It can be a liquid, a solid, or a gas. Water flowing from a faucet is liquid. Ice cubes are solid water. Water that disappears from a steaming teakettle is water vapor, which is a gas. Look around you, and you will see some of the many places where water can be found.

Minibook, page 1

The total amount of water on Earth does not change. However, water moves from place to place. Look at the clouds. They are made of tiny drops of water, light enough to float in the air. When there are enough tiny drops, they form a cloud. When the drops get heavy enough, they fall from the clouds. We call that rain. Rain is water in liquid form.

Minibook, page 2

When the temperature gets cold enough to freeze in winter, the water in the clouds falls as snowflakes. Snow is solid water. Ice is solid water, too. Ice is made when water freezes. Look at the mountaintops covered with snow and ice. Look at the skating pond below. They are cold and solid.

Minibook, page 3

Some rainwater soaks into the ground. Some of it flows into lakes, rivers, and streams. Snow and ice melt when the temperature gets warmer in spring. They melt into liquid water. Then the rivers take the water to the oceans. Look at the ocean. It holds water that was once rain, snow, or ice.

Minibook, page 4

After a rain, look down at the puddles. They don't stay around for long, because the water in them turns to vapor. We say the water evaporates. You cannot see water vapor in the air. Water vapor is a gas, and a gas is invisible.

Minibook, page 5

Living things need water to live and grow. Living things have water inside them. Inside a tree is sticky, watery sap. Even a cactus in a dry desert stores up water inside its stem. Orange and apple trees grow fruit with delicious watery juices inside. Your body is wet and watery inside. If you skin your knee, blood drips from the scrape, because blood is watery, too.

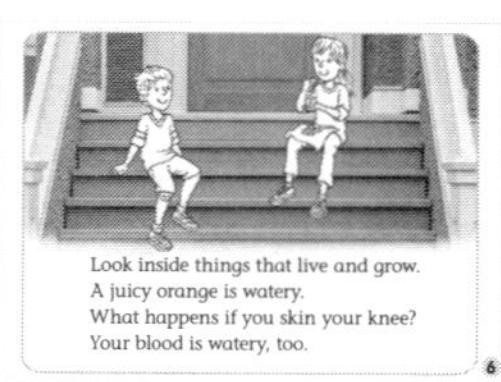

Minibook, page 6

Look at the rain clouds and mountaintops. Look at the ocean. Look at the puddles. Look inside living things. Some water is liquid and some is solid. Some water becomes an invisible gas. Water is in many places and in many forms.

Minibook, page 7

Name: _______________________________

Dictionary

Look at the picture. Read the word.
Write the word on the line.

Content Vocabulary

cloud

____

gas

____

liquid

____

melt

____

mountain

____

ocean

____

puddle

____

solid

____

Words to Know

cold	cover	enough	flows	happens
inside	rain	tiny	vapor	water

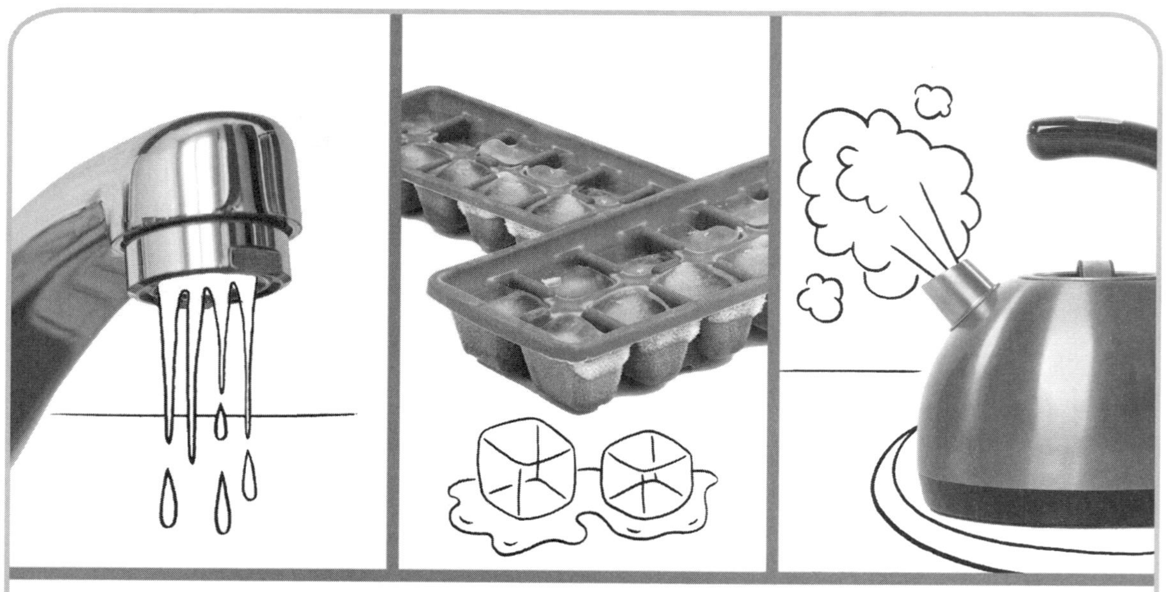

Where can you find water?
It can be a liquid, a solid, or a gas.
Let's look for water.

1

Look up at the clouds.
Clouds are made of tiny drops of water.
If the drops get big enough, they fall as rain.
Rain is liquid water.

2

Look up at the mountains.
Snow and ice cover the top of the mountains.
Snow and ice are solid water.
Cold makes water solid.

3

Look out at the ocean.
Rainwater flows into the ocean.
Snow and ice melt into liquid water.
This water flows into the ocean, too.

4

Look down at the puddles.
The puddles go away when
the water turns to vapor.
You cannot see water vapor in the air.
Water vapor is a gas.

5

Look inside things that live and grow.
A juicy orange is watery.
What happens if you skin your knee?
Your blood is watery, too.

6

Where can you find water?
Look up, out, down, or inside.
You can find water in many places.

7

I Read and Understand

Read and answer.

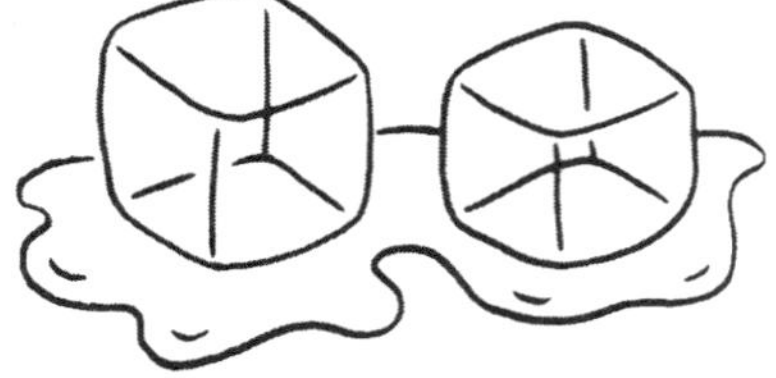

1. Clouds are ____.
   ○ water
   ○ inside

2. Snow is ____ water.
   ○ liquid
   ○ solid

3. Ice ____ into liquid water.
   ○ grows
   ○ melts

4. You cannot see water ____.
   ○ vapor
   ○ drops

5. Water can be solid, liquid, or ____.
   ○ gas
   ○ big

I Read Closely

Read. Mark the sentence that goes with the picture.

○ Look out at the ocean.

○ The puddles go away when the water turns to vapor.

○ It can be a liquid, a solid, or a gas.

○ Cold makes water solid.

○ Rain is liquid water.

○ A juicy orange is watery.

○ Snow and ice are solid water.

○ Water vapor is a gas.

Words I Know

Read and answer.

1. Water _____ into the ocean.
   - happens
   - flows
   - looks

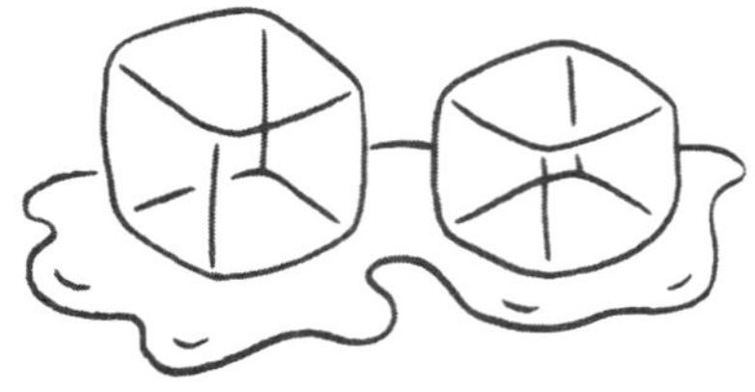

2. Rain is _____.
   - water
   - ocean
   - gas

3. The _____ went away.
   - mountain
   - puddle
   - ocean

4. Ice is a _____.
   - gas
   - mountain
   - solid

5. The ocean is _____ water.
   - vapor
   - solid
   - liquid

Name: _______________________

I Can Write

Think about what you read.
Write about each picture.

1. _______________________

____

2. _______________________

____

3. _______________________

____

Lesson Objective	Students will learn that the Statue of Liberty is a symbol of American values.
Content Knowledge	Citizenship includes an awareness of the symbols of our nation.

Lesson Preparation

Reproduce and distribute to each student one copy of the dictionary page (p. 57), the minibook pages (pp. 58–61), and the activity pages (pp. 62–65).

Student Minibook: Reproduce the minibook pages. Cut them in half and staple them together in numerical order to make an 8-page booklet.

Learn

1 Build Background

2 Introduce the Vocabulary
Dictionary

3 Read the Texts
The Statue of Liberty Minibook
Teacher's Complex Text

Analyze

4 Reading Comprehension Activities
I Read and Understand
I Read Closely

5 Close Reading Activity
Oral Discussion Questions

6 Vocabulary Activity
Words I Know

Write

7 Writing Activity
I Can Write

1 Build Background

Explain to students that a symbol is something that stands for something else. For example, sports teams have an animal such as a bear or a tiger. A flag is a symbol of our country. Other symbols of the United States include the bald eagle and the White House. Have students look around the classroom for symbols.

2 Introduce the Vocabulary

Content Vocabulary Point to each pictured word. Read the word aloud and have students echo you. Then have them write the word on the line. Explain any phonetic structures that are unfamiliar to your students. Discuss word meanings as needed.

Words to Know Point to each word and read it aloud. Have students echo you. Point out that the word *freedom* means that people can speak, do, and think as they wish without fear.

3 Read the Texts

Minibook Guide students in reading the minibook together aloud.

Teacher's Complex Text Have students look at the pictures in their minibooks as you read aloud the corresponding Teacher's Complex Text on page 56. Say: *Look at the pictures in your book as I read more information about the Statue of Liberty. Look at the picture on page 1. Listen as I read.*

4 Reading Comprehension Activities

Guide students through completing the activities on pages 62 and 63. Encourage them to look in their minibooks to find information.

5 Close Reading Activity

Oral Discussion Use the Oral Discussion Questions on the right to guide students in a discussion about what they have read and heard. Before you begin, make sure each student has colored pencils and his or her minibook.

Begin by reading aloud a question and having students answer the question and mark the answer in their minibooks.

6 Vocabulary Activity

Guide students through the vocabulary activity on page 64. After they finish, have them put an X next to another name for the Statue of Liberty.

7 Writing Activity

Guide students through the writing activity on page 65. Have them use information from their minibook and the Teacher's Complex Text. Their sentences should relate to the story. Then have volunteers read aloud their sentences.

Oral Discussion Questions

1. **What is another name for the Statue of Liberty?** (*Lady Liberty*) **Circle this name with green each place you see it.** (pages 1, 4, 5)

2. **Was France a friend to America? How do you know?** (*Yes, because the people of France gave America the Statue of Liberty.*) (page 2) **Make a red X next to the sentence that gives the answer.**

3. **What does the word *freedom* mean?** (*It means people can speak, think, and do as they wish.*) **Draw a blue line under the word *freedom* on page 3.**

4. **What symbols does the Statue of Liberty have?** (*a golden light*) (page 4) (*a broken chain*) (page 5) **Circle them with red.**

5. **Why was America growing? Read the sentences that tell why.** (*People came to America from around the world.*) (page 6) (*They knew America promised freedom.*) (page 7) **Draw a yellow line under the sentences.**

6. **Why is the Statue of Liberty important?** (*E.g., It is important because it is a symbol to the world of America's freedom. People in many lands do not have freedom as we do in America.*)

The Statue of Liberty

The Statue of Liberty stands tall in New York Harbor, on Liberty Island. The statue and its base measure almost 306 feet tall. The face of the statue is more than 8 feet tall! Its full name is the Statue of Liberty Enlightening the World, but many people call her Lady Liberty.

Minibook, page 1

The Statue of Liberty was a gift from the people of France to the people of the United States more than 125 years ago. It was carried across the Atlantic Ocean on the French ship *Isere* (ee-ZAIR). The 300 copper pieces of the statue were packed into 214 crates for the trip, and the ship almost sank in rough seas. The pieces were not put together until the base was built, almost a year after the statue arrived in New York. The Statue of Liberty was dedicated on October 28, 1886.

Minibook, page 2

A sculptor is an artist who creates statues. Frederic Bartholdi was the French artist who designed the Statue of Liberty. His dream of making a colossal statue took many years to come true. Bartholdi wanted the statue to be a symbol of freedom and democracy.

Minibook, page 3

The Statue of Liberty became a symbol of freedom for the whole world. The statue itself has many symbols, too. Lady Liberty holds high a torch with a golden flame. The flame is a symbol of lighting the way to liberty and freedom.

Minibook, page 4

There is another symbol at the foot of the statue. Lady Liberty has a broken chain wrapped around her feet. Lady Liberty steps forward out of the chain. This is a symbol of freedom for people everywhere. Liberty is a powerful idea in the world.

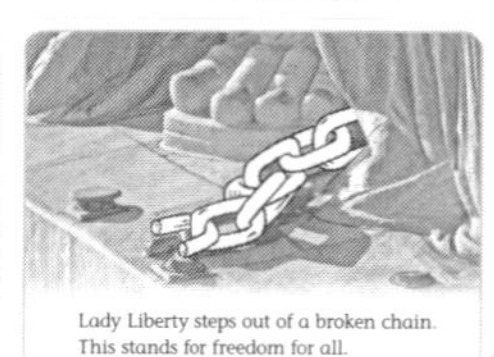

Minibook, page 5

In the 1800s and 1900s, when the Statue of Liberty was new, thousands of people were coming to America from around the world. Many of the people were poor, even though they worked hard. Many of them had suffered because of unfair laws. They had been treated badly in their own lands. They were looking for a better life.

Minibook, page 6

As they sailed into New York Harbor, these people saw the Statue of Liberty with her arm raised. They knew that America promised them liberty. In America, they could be free to speak, think, and do as they wished. They could be free from fear. They could have a better life.

Minibook, page 7

Name: _______________________

Dictionary

Look at the picture. Read the word.
Write the word on the line.

Content Vocabulary

America

____

artist

____

boxes

____

chain

____

light

____

ship

____

statue

____

world

____

Words to Know

broken   freedom   golden

liberty   promised

57

The Statue of Liberty

Name: ________________

The Statue of Liberty stands tall.
Sometimes it is called Lady Liberty.

1

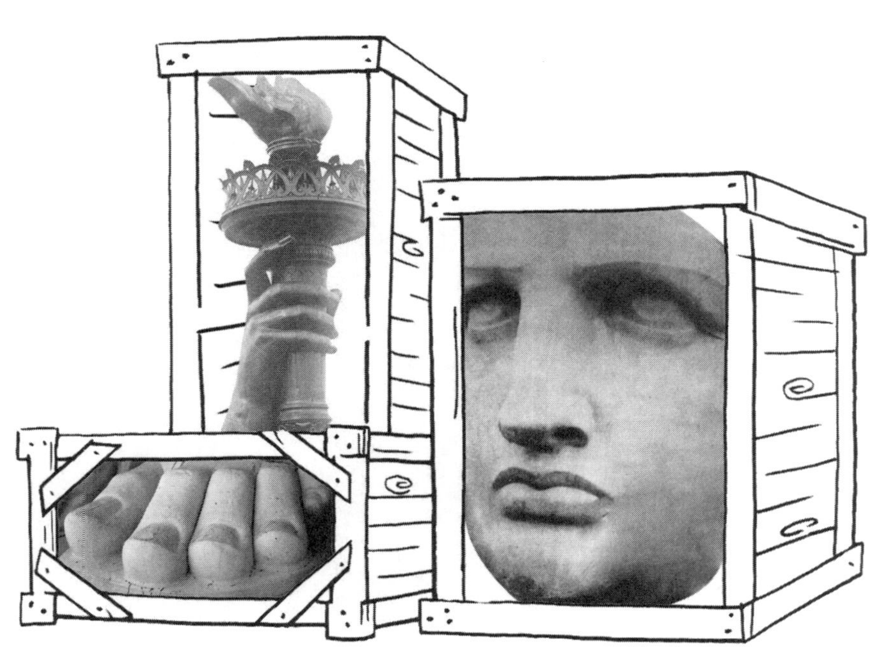

France gave the statue to America.
It came in pieces, in boxes, on a ship.

2

An artist made the Statue of Liberty.
He wanted it to stand for freedom.

3

Lady Liberty holds a golden light.
It lights the way to freedom.

4

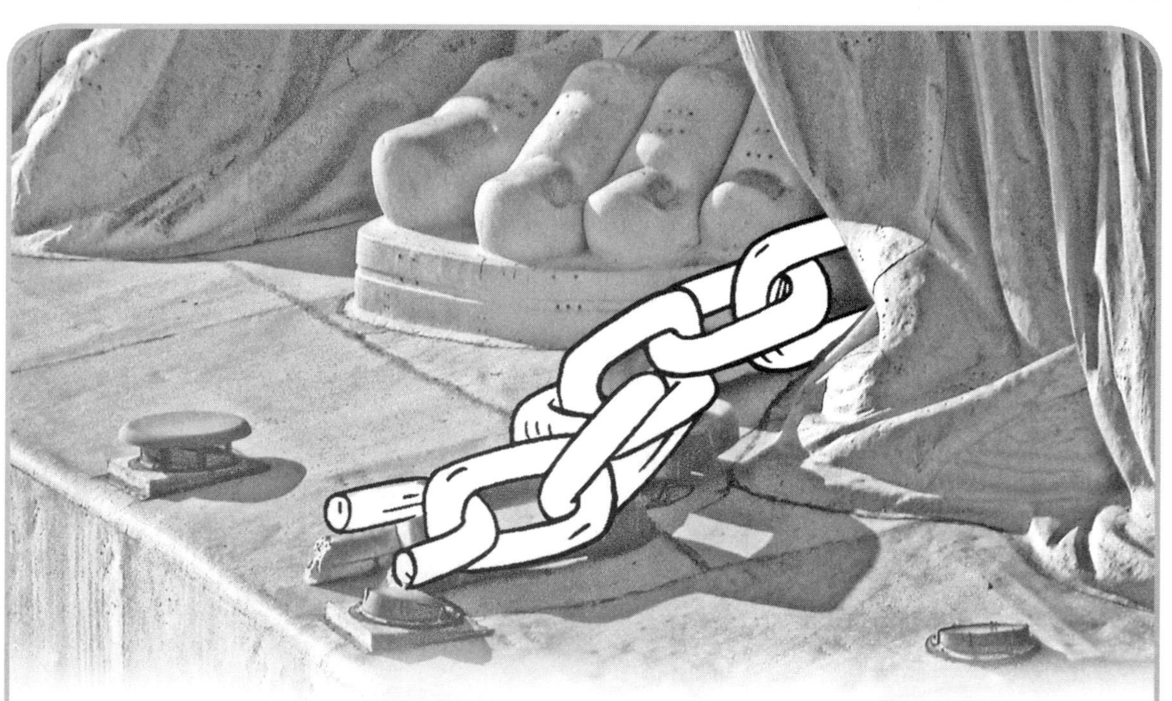

Lady Liberty steps out of a broken chain.
This stands for freedom for all.

5

People came to America from around the world.
Many were poor and suffering.

6

They saw the Statue of Liberty.
They knew America promised freedom.

7

Name: _______________________________

I Read and Understand

Read and answer.

1. The statue is called ____.
   - ○ Lady Liberty
   - ○ Lady Freedom

2. The statue came from the people of ____.
   - ○ America
   - ○ France

3. The light shows the way ____.
   - ○ to freedom
   - ○ people were poor

4. The broken chain is for ____.
   - ○ freedom for all
   - ○ a ship

5. Think about the Statue of Liberty.
   Circle the words that tell about it.

America	lady	small
freedom	man	tall

Name: _______________________

I Read Closely

Read. Mark the sentence that goes with the picture.

- ○ An artist made the Statue of Liberty.
- ○ The Statue of Liberty stands tall.

- ○ It lights the way to freedom.
- ○ Lady Liberty steps out of a broken chain.

- ○ It came in pieces, in boxes, on a ship.
- ○ The Statue of Liberty stands tall.

- ○ Many were poor and suffering.
- ○ They saw the Statue of Liberty.

Name: _______________________________

Words I Know

Read and answer.

1. Lady Liberty is a _____.
   - ○ ship
   - ○ light
   - ○ statue

2. We see the Statue of _____.
   - ○ France
   - ○ Liberty
   - ○ America

3. The chain is _____.
   - ○ broken
   - ○ golden
   - ○ boxes

4. You can go by _____.
   - ○ world
   - ○ ship
   - ○ chain

5. America has _____.
   - ○ freedom
   - ○ world
   - ○ light

Name: ___________________________________

I Can Write

Write the words to finish the sentence.

Word Box

stands for freedom	came to America
Statue of Liberty	shows the way

1. The _________________________ stands tall.

2. A golden light _________________________ to freedom.

3. A broken chain _________________________.

4. Many people _________________________.

Write your own sentence about the Statue of Liberty.

____

____

Social Studies
Looking at the United States

Lesson Objective Students will understand that a United States map shows us the physical boundaries of the states and the country.

Content Knowledge Places can be located on maps; maps serve as representations of places, physical features, and objects.

Lesson Preparation

Reproduce and distribute to each student one copy of the dictionary page (p. 69), the minibook pages (pp. 70–73), and the activity pages (pp. 74–77).

Student Minibook: Reproduce the minibook pages. Cut them in half and staple them together in numerical order to make an 8-page booklet.

Learn

1 Build Background

2 Introduce the Vocabulary
Dictionary

3 Read the Texts
Looking at the United States Minibook
Teacher's Complex Text

Analyze

4 Reading Comprehension Activities
I Read and Understand
I Read Closely

5 Close Reading Activity
Oral Discussion Questions

6 Vocabulary Activity
Words I Know

Write

7 Writing Activity
I Can Write

1 Build Background

Explain to students that a map is a drawing of a place as if seen from above. A map shows where things or places are located. A map is different from a globe because a map is a flat picture and a globe is round like a ball.

2 Introduce the Vocabulary

Content Vocabulary Point to each pictured word. Read the word aloud and have students echo you. Then have them write the word on the line. For the word *border*, have students use one finger to trace the outline of the state. Explain any phonetic structures that are unfamiliar to your students. Discuss word meanings as needed.

Words to Know Point to each word and read it aloud. Have students echo you. Explain that the word *state* can mean "a place where people live and vote to elect a government" or "to say something clearly."

3 Read the Texts

Minibook Guide students in reading the minibook together aloud.

Teacher's Complex Text Have students look at the pictures in their minibooks as you read aloud the corresponding Teacher's Complex Text on page 68. Say: *Look at the pictures in your book as I read you more information about the map of the United States. Look at the picture on page 1. Listen as I read.*

4 Reading Comprehension Activities

Guide students through completing the activities on pages 74 and 75. Encourage them to look in their minibooks to find information.

5 Close Reading Activity

Oral Discussion Use the Oral Discussion Questions on the right to guide students in a discussion about what they have read and heard. Before you begin, make sure each student has colored pencils and his or her minibook.

Begin by reading aloud a question and having students answer the question and mark the answer in their minibooks.

6 Vocabulary Activity

Guide students through the vocabulary activity on page 76. After they finish, ask them to find the words *United States* on the page and circle them with green.

7 Writing Activity

Guide students through the writing activity on page 77. Have them use information from their minibook and the Teacher's Complex Text. Their sentences should relate to the story. Then have volunteers read aloud their sentences.

Oral Discussion Questions

1. **What is the title of the book?** (*Looking at the United States*) **Draw a green line under the title.** (title page)

2. **The United States is made up of states of different sizes and shapes. How many states are there?** (*50*) **Circle the number with blue.** (page 2)

3. **Page 4 says that lines that divide the states are called borders. Make a red X on the state of South Dakota. Trace its borders with red.** (*a red X on South Dakota, with red borders*) (page 4)

4. **Look at the state shapes on page 3. Trace the borders of Texas with purple. Trace the borders of Florida with green. Which of those two states has the longer border?** (*Texas*) (page 3)

5. **What is the largest state?** (*Alaska*) **Circle its name with green.** (page 5)

6. **What fact could you tell someone about Rhode Island?** (*It is the smallest state. It shares a border with two other states.*) **Color Rhode Island orange.** (page 6)

7. **What is the name of your state? With how many other states does it share a border? Color your state using your favorite color.** (*Answers may vary.*)

Looking at the United States

The United States is a big country. You can see the shape of the United States by looking at the map. The compass rose at the bottom of the map shows four directions: N stands for north, S for south, E for east, and W for west.

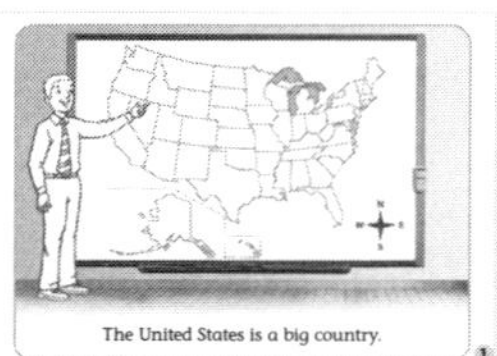

Minibook, page 1

The United States is a country made up of 50 states. The United States map shows the location of each state. A location is where something is. Forty-eight of the states are connected. The states of Alaska and Hawaii are part of the United States, but they are not connected.

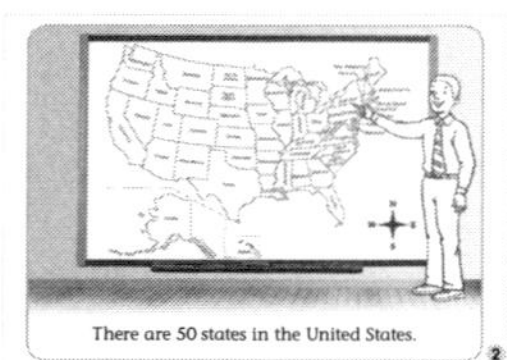

Minibook, page 2

Each state has a different shape, and the states are all different sizes, too. This picture shows the different shapes and sizes of some of the states. California and Texas are larger than New York, Florida, and Michigan.

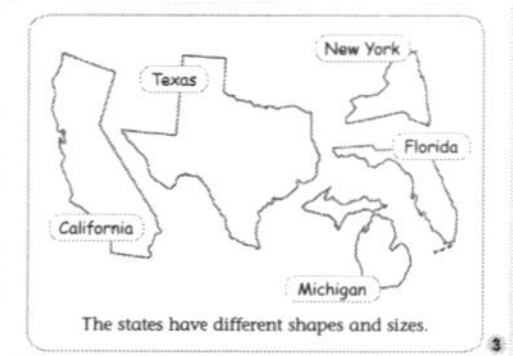

Minibook, page 3

The lines that divide, or separate, the states are called borders. The borders give each state its very own shape, so it looks different from the others. Most states share a border with two, three, or more states.

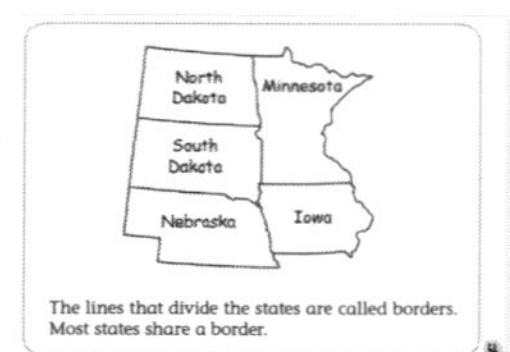

Minibook, page 4

The state of Alaska is the largest state. Alaska is part of the United States, but it does not share a border with any other state. Although Alaska is huge, fewer people live there than in most other states. Alaska's nickname is "The Last Frontier," because it has lots of open land to be explored.

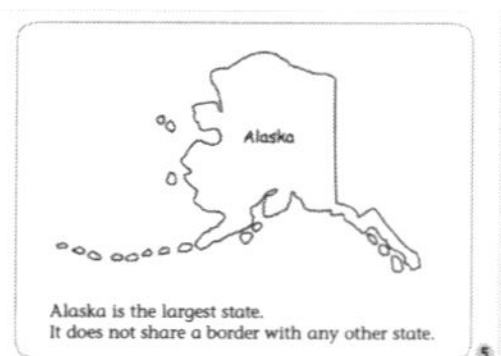

Minibook, page 5

The state of Rhode Island is the smallest state. Because of its size, the state is often called "Little Rhody." It is in the eastern part of the United States. Rhode Island shares a border with two other states. They are Massachusetts and Connecticut.

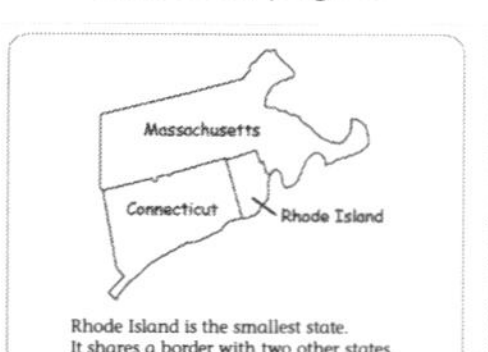

Minibook, page 6

Your state is one of the 50 states of the United States. Locate your state on the map of the United States. Look carefully at the shape of your state. Then draw it. What is the name of your state? Write your state's name under your picture.

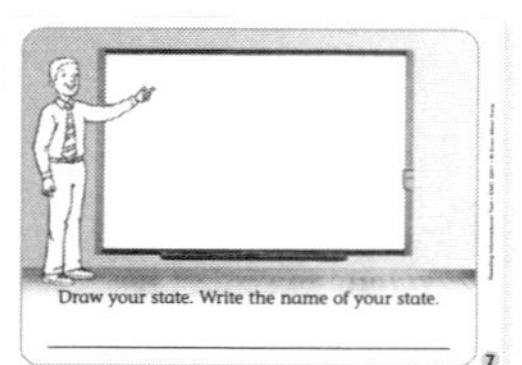

Minibook, page 7

Name: _______________________________

Dictionary

Look at the picture. Read the word.
Write the word on the line.

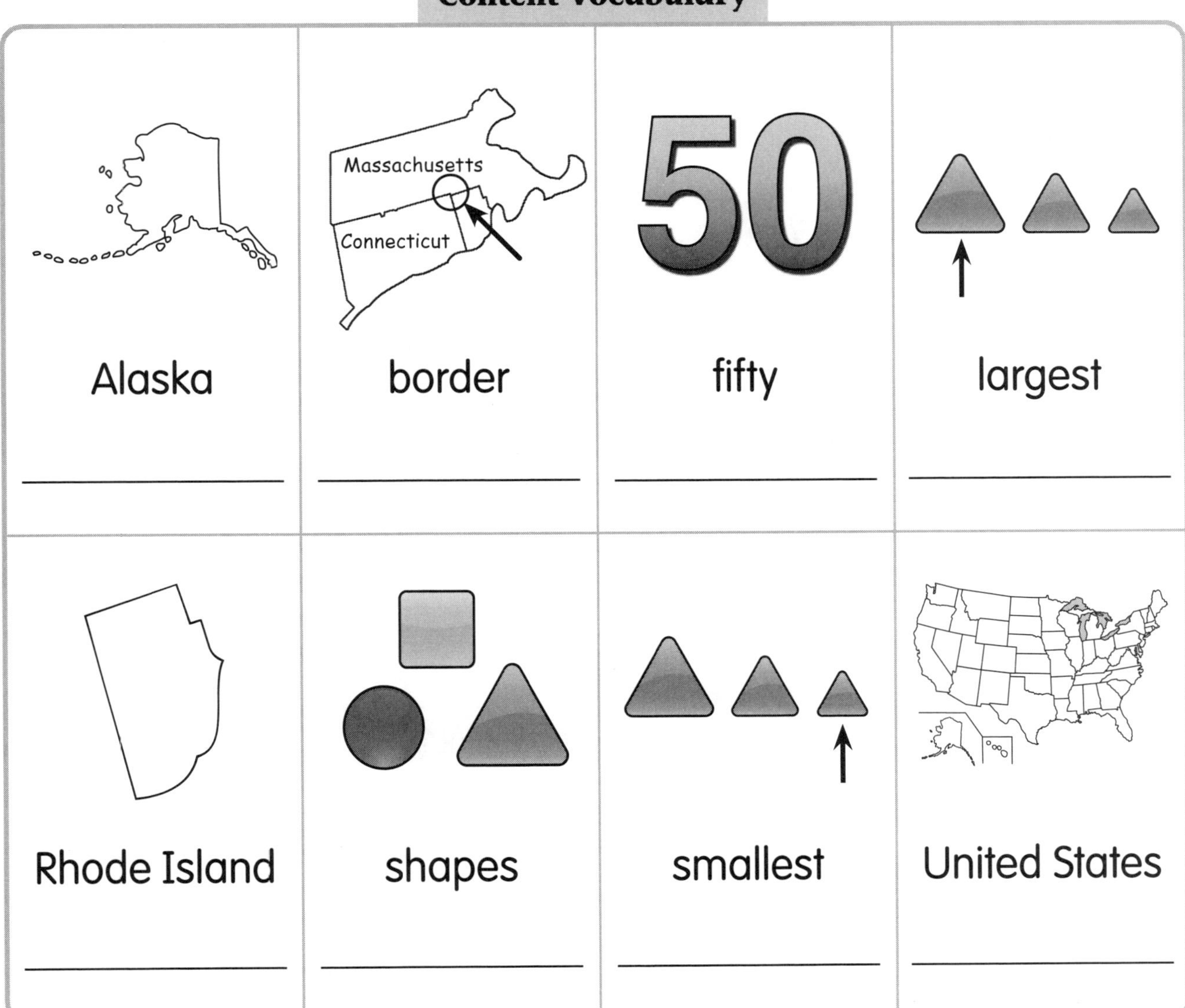

Looking at the United States

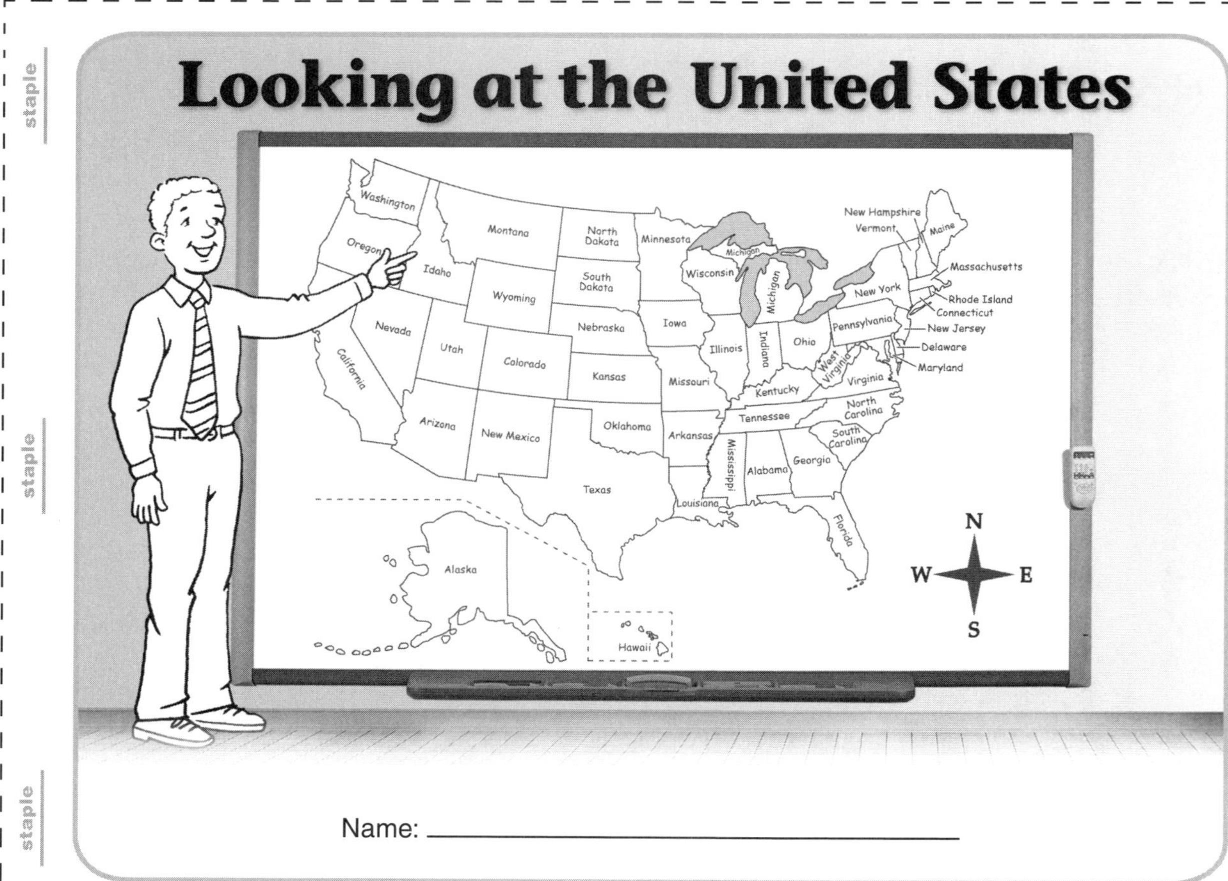

Name: _______________________

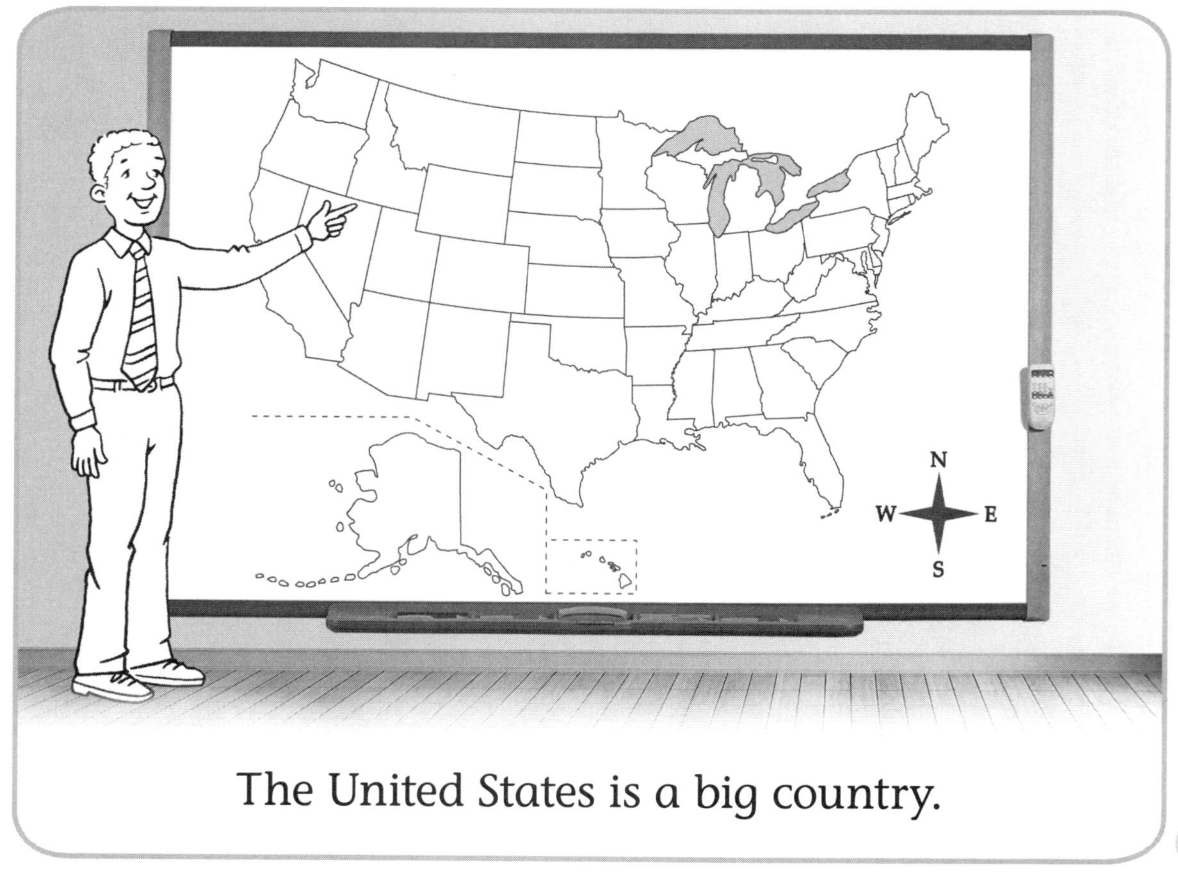

The United States is a big country.

Reading Comprehension: Nonfiction • EMC 3261 • © Evan-Moor Corporation

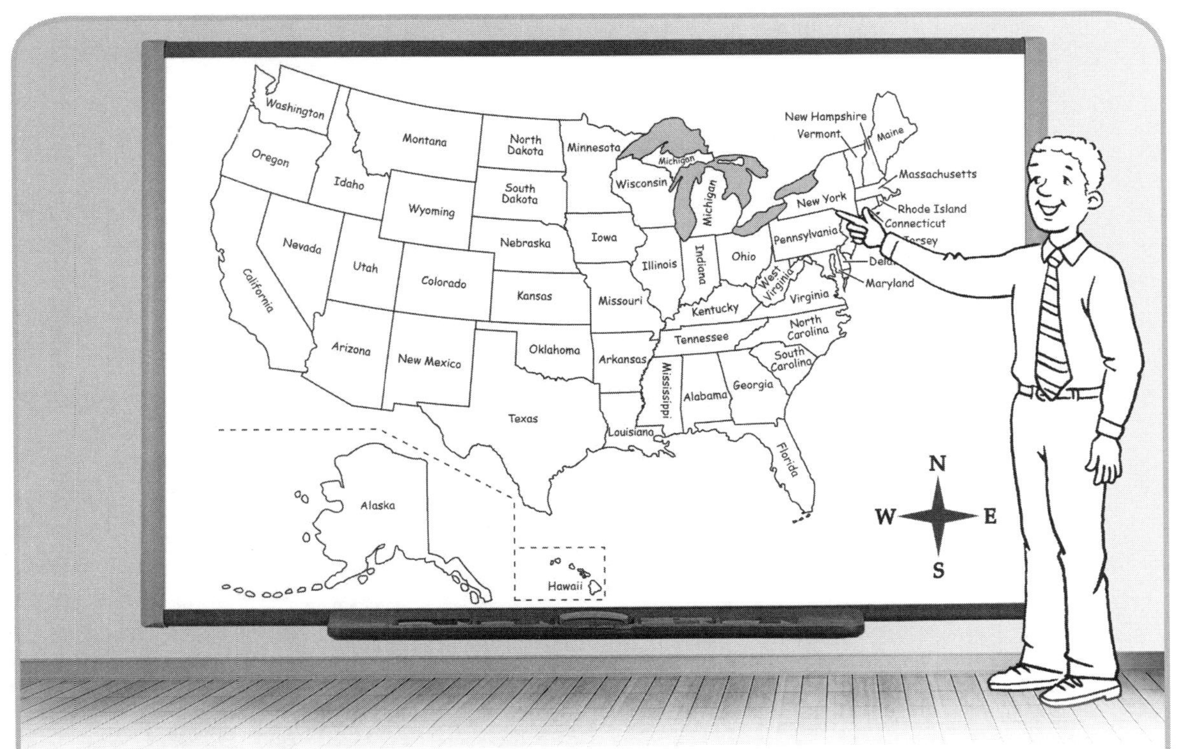

There are 50 states in the United States.

2

The states have different shapes and sizes.

3

The lines that divide the states are called borders.
Most states share a border.

4

Alaska is the largest state.
It does not share a border with any other state.

5

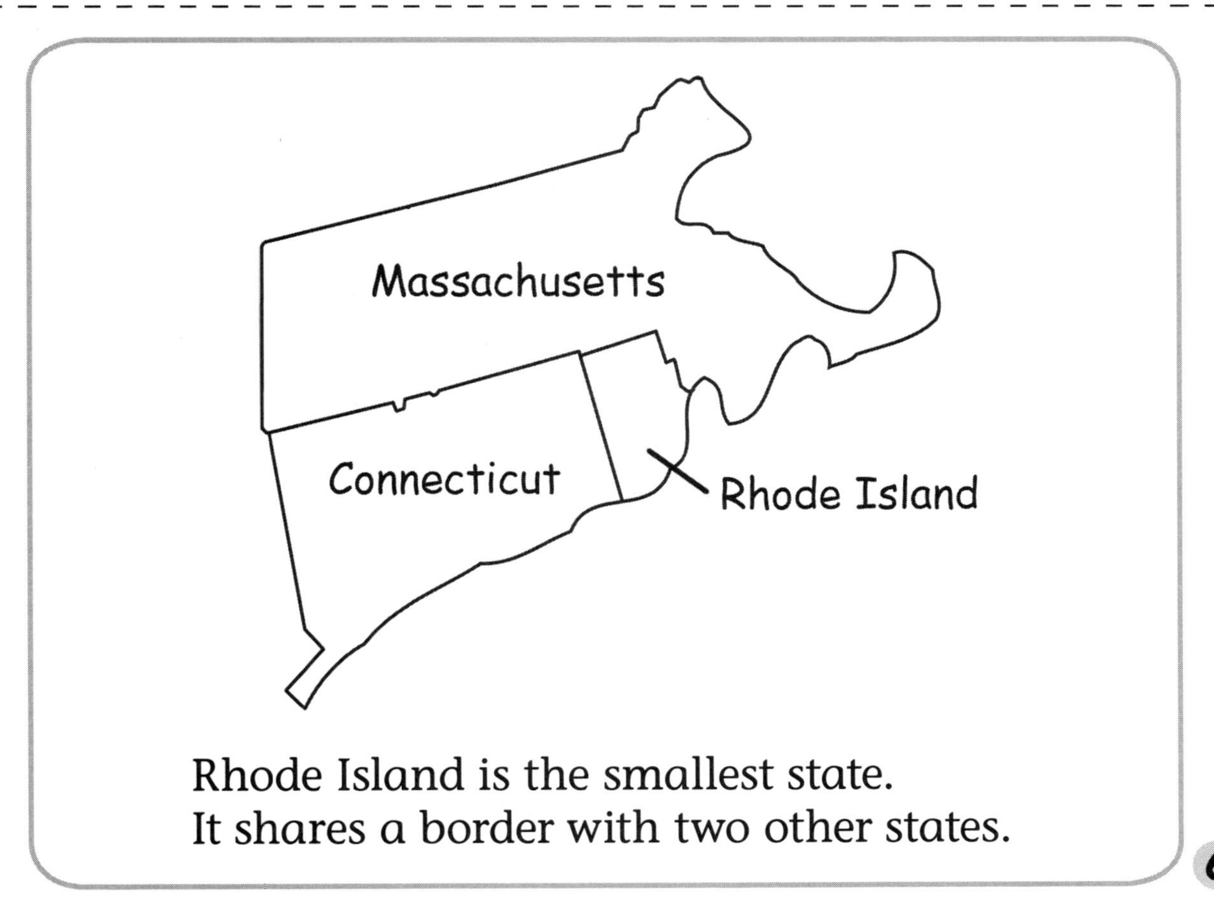

Rhode Island is the smallest state.
It shares a border with two other states.

6

Draw your state. Write the name of your state.

7

Reading Comprehension: Nonfiction • EMC 3261 • © Evan-Moor Corporation

I Read and Understand

Read and answer.

1. ____ is a country.
   - ○ The United States
   - ○ California

2. The United States has ____.
   - ○ 100 states
   - ○ 50 states

3. Alaska is the ____ state.
   - ○ smallest
   - ○ largest

4. Rhode Island is the ____ state.
   - ○ smallest
   - ○ largest

5. Most states share a ____.
   - ○ shape
   - ○ border

   Reading Comprehension: Nonfiction • EMC 3261 • © Evan-Moor Corporation

Name: _______________________

I Read Closely

Read. Mark the sentence that goes with the picture.

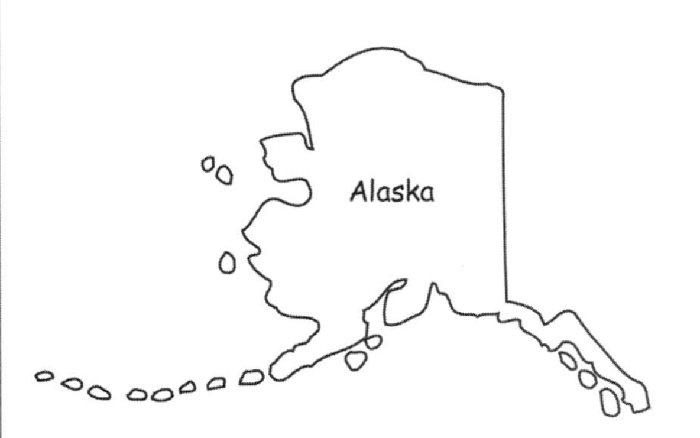

○ The United States is a big country.

○ Alaska is the largest state.

○ Most states share a border.

○ There are 50 states in the United States.

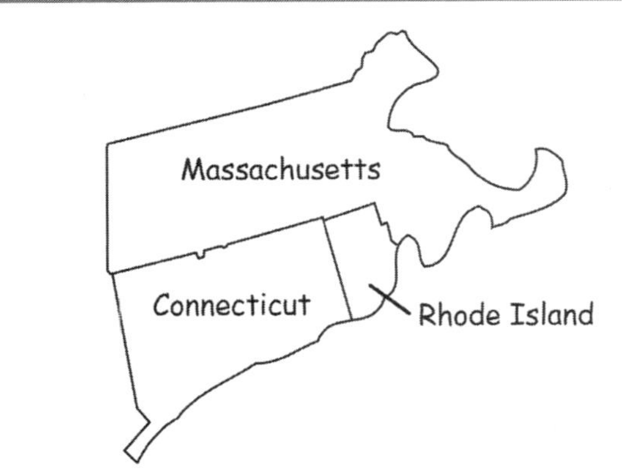

○ It does not share a border with any other state.

○ It shares a border with two other states.

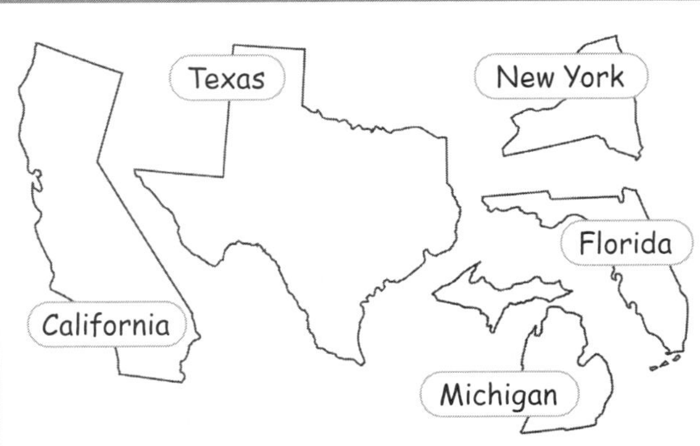

○ The states have different shapes and sizes.

○ Rhode Island is the smallest state.

Name: _______________________________

Words I Know

Read and answer.

1. Each state has a ____.
   - ○ smallest
   - ○ share
   - ○ shape

2. The states have ____ sizes.
   - ○ different
   - ○ divide
   - ○ border

3. There are ____ states.
   - ○ country
   - ○ fifty
   - ○ size

4. Your ____ is on the map.
   - ○ fifty
   - ○ state
   - ○ divide

5. It is a map of the ____.
   - ○ United States
   - ○ different
   - ○ largest

Reading Comprehension: Nonfiction • EMC 3261 • © Evan-Moor Corporation

Name: _______________________

I Can Write

Write the words to finish the sentence.

Word Box

any other state	two other states
have different shapes	divide the states

1. The fifty states ________________________.

2. Rhode Island shares a border with ________________

   ________________________.

3. Alaska does not share a border with ______________

   ________________________.

4. Borders are lines that ____________________.

Write your own sentence about your state's borders.

____

____

Biography
Winslow Homer, American Artist

Lesson Objective Students will understand that art shows different times and places and that Winslow Homer's art shows people and places from more than 100 years ago.

Content Knowledge Art helps us understand human experiences both past and present.

Lesson Preparation

Reproduce and distribute to each student one copy of the dictionary page (p. 81), the minibook pages (pp. 82–85), and the activity pages (pp. 86–89).

Student Minibook: Reproduce the minibook pages. Cut them in half and staple them together in numerical order to make an 8-page booklet.

Learn

1 Build Background

2 Introduce the Vocabulary
Dictionary

3 Read the Texts
Winslow Homer, American Artist Minibook
Teacher's Complex Text

Analyze

4 Reading Comprehension Activities
I Read and Understand
I Read Closely

5 Close Reading Activity
Oral Discussion Questions

6 Vocabulary Activity
Words I Know

Write

7 Writing Activity
I Can Write

1 Build Background

Explain to students that artists make art about many things. For example, a painting might show children playing or animals in a field. An artist organizes the things shown in a painting. The colors, lines, shapes, and space in a painting can give it a mood, or feeling. A painting can tell a story.

2 Introduce the Vocabulary

Content Vocabulary Point to each pictured word. Read the word aloud and have students echo you. Then have them write the word on the line. Explain any phonetic structures that are unfamiliar to your students. Discuss word meanings as needed.

Words to Know Point to each word and read it aloud. Have students echo you. Point out that *country* can mean "an area outside of a city" or "a large area of land with its own rules."

3 Read the Texts

Minibook Guide students in reading the minibook together aloud.

Teacher's Complex Text Have students look at the pictures in their minibooks as you read aloud the corresponding Teacher's Complex Text on page 80. Say: *Look at the pictures in your book as I read you more information about Winslow Homer. Look at the picture on page 1. Listen as I read.* Optional: Display color reproductions of the paintings as you read the text.

4 Reading Comprehension Activities

Guide students through completing the activities on pages 86 and 87. Encourage them to look in their minibooks to find information.

5 Close Reading Activity

Oral Discussion Use the Oral Discussion Questions on the right to guide students in a discussion about what they have read and heard. Before you begin, make sure each student has colored pencils and his or her minibook.

Begin by reading aloud a question and having students answer the question and mark the answer in their minibooks.

6 Vocabulary Activity

Guide students through the vocabulary activity on page 88. After they finish, have them circle the two words with *ing* at the end.

7 Writing Activity

Guide students through the writing activity on page 89. Have them use information from their minibook and the Teacher's Complex Text. Their sentences should relate to the story. Then have volunteers read aloud their sentences.

Oral Discussion Questions

1. **Who is this book about?** (*Winslow Homer*) **Circle the title with purple.** (title page) **Who was he?** (*an American artist*)

2. **When did Winslow Homer live?** (*1836 to 1910*) **Draw a red circle around the dates. What is he wearing?** (*a suit, tie or scarf, and hat*) **Color his hat blue.** (page 1)

3. **What are the boys doing in the painting "Snap the Whip"?** (*playing a game*) **Where are they?** (*on the grass; in the country*) **How did boys dress in those days?** (*E.g., They have hats, suspenders, and no shoes.*) **Color the boys' shirts.** (page 2)

4. **Where is the girl with the hay rake?** (*on a farm, in the country*) **Where do you think she is going?** (*home from the fields*) **How does she seem to feel?** (*E.g., tired*) **Color the trees green.** (page 3)

5. **What does the country school look like?** (*E.g., benches instead of desks, no computers*) **Color the teacher's desk orange.** (page 4)

6. **Does the girl in "The New Novel" look like she likes to read? Why or why not?** (*E.g., She is lying down reading her book; she seems very interested in what she is reading.*) **Color the girl's hair and dress red.** (page 5)

7. **Who is in the painting "Waiting for Dad"?** (*a boy, a mom, and a baby*) **Where do you think Dad is?** (*at sea on a boat; fishing*) (page 6)

Winslow Homer, American Artist

Winslow Homer was an American artist who lived from 1836 to 1910. Many people think he is the most important American painter of his time. Winslow's first art teacher was his mother. After high school, Winslow had jobs creating art for magazines. In 1867, Winslow Homer went to France for a year. While he was there, he practiced his painting. By 1875, many people liked his work.

Minibook, page 1

Winslow Homer liked to paint children playing. He painted *Snap the Whip* in 1872. This painting shows boys playing a game of snap-the-whip on the playground. The boys hold hands, run, and pull each other, and the last boy "snaps" off the end. The boys are barefoot, and they all wear hats.

Minibook, page 2

Winslow Homer also liked to paint pictures about farm life. He painted *Girl with Hay Rake* in 1878. Winslow Homer used watercolors on paper to paint this picture of a farm girl. She is wearing a bonnet and holding a hay rake that she uses to collect hay.

Minibook, page 3

Winslow Homer liked to paint children at school. His painting called *The Country School* shows a busy one-room school. All the grades are in one classroom. The children work at long tables and sit on benches. Look carefully to see the teacher's hat hung above the chalkboard.

Minibook, page 4

In his painting called *The New Novel*, Winslow Homer painted a young woman quietly reading a novel on a summer day. A novel is a chapter book. Homer painted the young woman in a colorful red dress.

Minibook, page 5

For many years, Winslow Homer lived near the sea. It became one of his favorite things to paint. In *Waiting for Dad*, we can see a young boy in a hat sitting atop a boat on the shore. He is staring out to sea, watching for his father to come home.

Minibook, page 6

Breezing Up is one of Winslow Homer's most famous paintings. In it, a father and three boys are sailing. They look like they are enjoying the ride. We can see the breeze in the sails, the tilt of the boat, and choppy waves. Their hat brims turn up in the breeze. When we look at the paintings of Winslow Homer, we can see how some children lived long ago. We can see women at work and at rest. We can see how people lived by the sea. We learn what American life was like for some people in days gone by.

Minibook, page 7

Name: __________________________

Dictionary

Look at the picture. Read the word.
Write the word on the line.

Content Vocabulary

American

____

novel

____

painter

____

painting

____

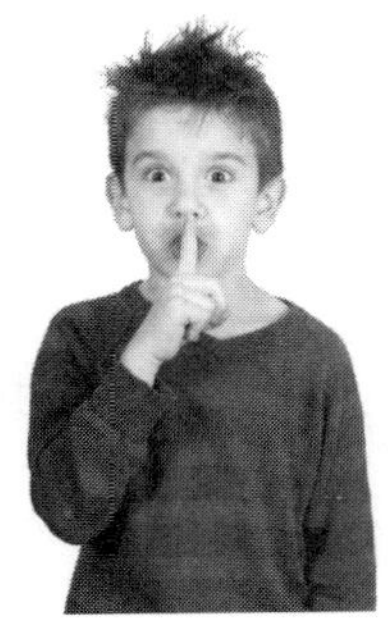

quiet

____

rake

____

sea

____

time

____

Words to Know

breezing	country	gone
show	some	whip

Winslow Homer
American Artist

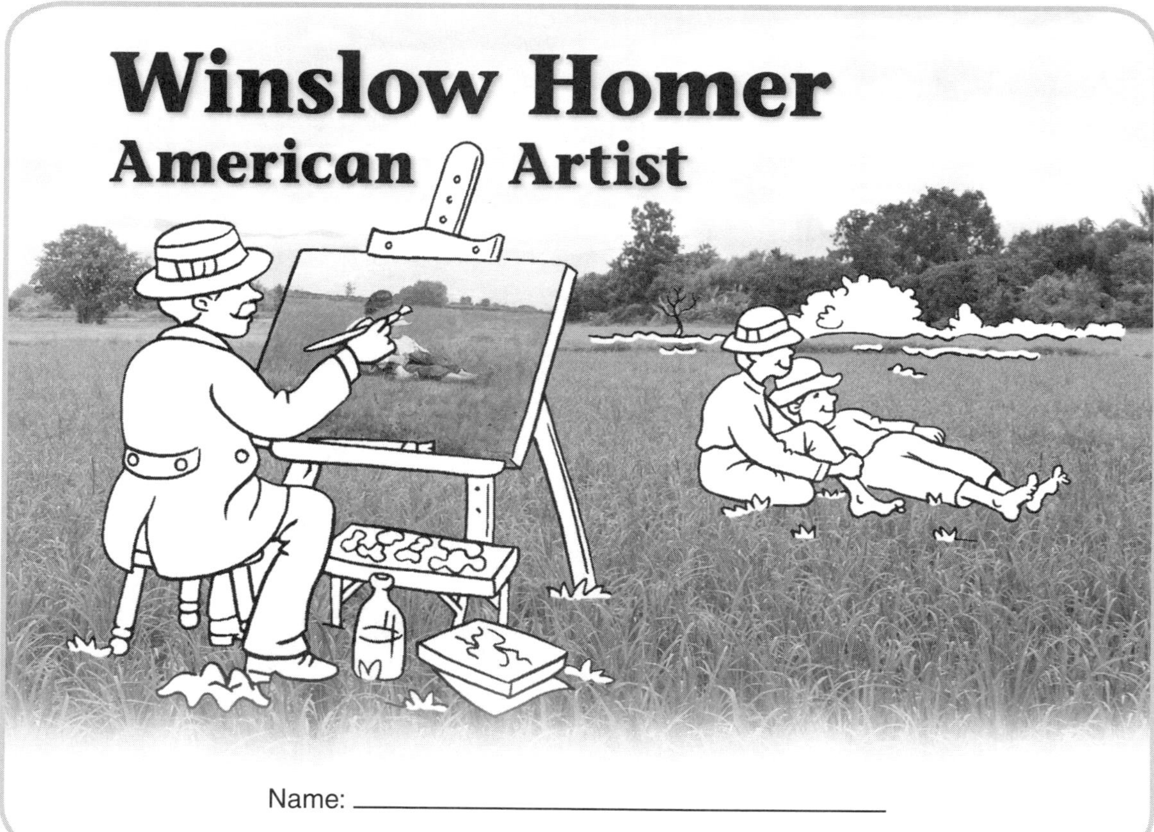

Name: _______________________

Winslow Homer was an American painter.

1

Some of his paintings show play time.

2

Some of his paintings show work time.

3

Some of his paintings show school time.

4

Some of his paintings show quiet times.

5

Some of his paintings show times by the sea.

6

The paintings of Winslow Homer show us what life was like in times gone by.

7

Reading Comprehension: Nonfiction • EMC 3261 • © Evan-Moor Corporation

BIOGRAPHY

Winslow Homer,
American Artist

I Read and Understand

Read and answer.

1. Winslow Homer was a ____.
   - ○ painting
   - ○ painter

2. Each painting has ____.
   - ○ the same name
   - ○ a different name

3. Winslow Homer often painted the ____.
   - ○ sea
   - ○ mountains

4. The paintings are about ____.
   - ○ people
   - ○ animals

5. The paintings show ____.
   - ○ life today
   - ○ times gone by

Name: ___________________

I Read Closely

Read. Mark the sentence that goes with the picture.

○ The Country School
○ The New Novel

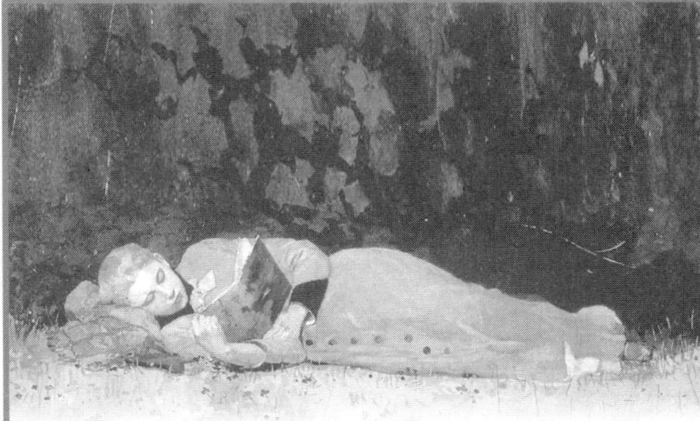

○ Girl with Hay Rake
○ The New Novel

○ Breezing Up
○ Snap the Whip

○ The Country School
○ Waiting for Dad

Words I Know

Read and answer.

1. It is _____ when I read.
   - ○ quiet
   - ○ some
   - ○ rake

2. A boat is on the _____.
   - ○ rake
   - ○ time
   - ○ sea

3. The lady reads a _____.
   - ○ gone
   - ○ novel
   - ○ show

4. We are _____.
   - ○ American
   - ○ country
   - ○ whip

5. A _____ makes art.
   - ○ painter
   - ○ painting
   - ○ breezing

I Can Write

Write the words to finish the sentence.

Word Box

work time	times by the sea
was a painter	school time

1. Winslow Homer _______________________________.

2. The painting *Girl with Hay Rake* shows _______________

    _______________________________.

3. The painting *The Country School* shows _______________

    _______________________________.

4. The painting *Breezing Up* shows _______________

    _______________________________.

Choose a Winslow Homer painting. Write a sentence about it.

____

____

Biography
Maria Martinez, Native American Potter

Lesson Objective   Students will understand that families can teach each other about how life used to be by making things.

Content Knowledge   Understanding the way people used to live helps us shape the way we live today.

Lesson Preparation

Reproduce and distribute to each student one copy of the dictionary page (p. 93), the minibook pages (pp. 94–97), and the activity pages (pp. 98–101).

Student Minibook: Reproduce the minibook pages. Cut them in half and staple them together in numerical order to make an 8-page booklet.

Learn

1 Build Background

2 Introduce the Vocabulary
Dictionary

3 Read the Texts
Maria Martinez, Native American Potter
  Minibook
Teacher's Complex Text

Analyze

4 Reading Comprehension Activities
I Read and Understand
I Read Closely

5 Close Reading Activity
Oral Discussion Questions

6 Vocabulary Activity
Words I Know

Write

7 Writing Activity
I Can Write

1 Build Background

Explain to students that Native American peoples lived in many places all across the United States and spoke many different languages. Native Americans used the gifts of nature for their food, clothing, and shelter. For example, plants were used to make baskets, and clay was used to make pots. Shelter and clothing were made from animal skins.

2 Introduce the Vocabulary

Content Vocabulary Point to each pictured word. Read the word aloud and have students echo you. Then have them write the word on the line. Explain any phonetic structures that are unfamiliar to your students. Discuss word meanings as needed.

Words to Know Point to each word and read it aloud. Have students echo you. Point out the words that end in *-ed*.

3 Read the Texts

Minibook Guide students in reading the minibook together aloud.

Teacher's Complex Text Have students look at the pictures in their minibooks as you read aloud the corresponding Teacher's Complex Text on page 92. Say: *Look at the pictures in your book as I read you more information about the famous Native American potter Maria Martinez. Look at the picture on page 1. Listen as I read.*

4 Reading Comprehension Activities

Guide students through completing the activities on pages 98 and 99. Encourage them to look in their minibooks to find information.

5 Close Reading Activity

Oral Discussion Use the Oral Discussion Questions on the right to guide students in a discussion about what they have read and heard. Before you begin, make sure each student has colored pencils and his or her minibook.

Begin by reading aloud a question and having students answer the question and mark the answer in their minibooks.

6 Vocabulary Activity

Guide students through the vocabulary activity on page 100. After they finish, ask them to find and circle three words that could describe a pot. (clay, new, metal)

7 Writing Activity

Guide students through the writing activity on page 101. Have them use information from their minibook and the Teacher's Complex Text. Their sentences should relate to the story. Then have volunteers read aloud their sentences.

Oral Discussion Questions

1. **Who is this book about?** (*Maria Martinez*) **Make a blue dot next to her name.** (title page)

2. **What does the word** *pueblo* **mean?** (*town*) **Circle the word** *town* **with green.** (page 1)

3. **How did Maria learn to make pots?** (*She watched her aunt.*) **Make a red X next to the sentence that tells you.** (page 2)

4. **What did the railroad bring to Maria's pueblo?** (*metal pots, new people*) **Circle the words with orange. What did the new people think of Maria's pots?** (*They thought they were beautiful and they bought them.*) (page 3)

5. **How did Maria and Julian work together?** (*They made pots together; she shaped the clay and he painted the pots.*) **Draw a purple line under the words that tell you.** (page 4)

6. **What did Maria's pots look like?** (*shiny, black, some had pictures on them*) **Make a black dot next to each sentence that tells you.** (page 6)

7. **How could you summarize this story about Maria Martinez?** (*E.g., Maria learned from her aunt how to make pots. She studied very old pots to learn how they were made. Throughout her life, Maria worked to perfect the art of making beautiful pots. She handed down her knowledge to her family.*)

Maria Martinez, Native American Potter

Maria Martinez was born about 125 years ago in a little pueblo called San Ildefonso. A pueblo is a small town that was settled by Native Americans long ago. A pueblo has homes made of adobe, which is a type of mud brick. Today, Maria's pueblo is in the state of New Mexico, though it wasn't a state at the time Maria was born. Maria's people were Pueblo Indians, and their language was Tewa.

Minibook, page 1

The Pueblo people used the earth's gifts for their needs. They used the corn that grew in the earth for their food. They used the clay they found for making pots. The pots were used for cooking and storing things. Because they were used every day, the pots were decorated with beautiful designs. When she was a child, Maria watched her aunt Nicolasa make pots, and that is how Maria learned to make pots.

Minibook, page 2

Maria was young when the railroad first came to New Mexico from the East. The railroad was new, and it brought many new things with it, such as metal pots. People began to use the new cooking pots made of metal, so they did not need as many clay pots. The railroad brought visitors, too. These visitors wanted to buy the beautifully decorated clay pots they saw, and so the Pueblo people began to make pots to sell.

Minibook, page 3

When Maria was a young woman, she married Julian, and together they made pots to sell. Maria knew where the best clay was for her pots. She and Julian dug up the clay and mixed it with sand. Maria added water and shaped her pots from this mixture. Then Julian painted the pots. After the pots dried, Maria and Julian built a fire and carefully placed the pots inside of it to harden them.

Minibook, page 4

Some people who worked for a museum discovered ancient pots buried near the pueblos. Maria studied these pots carefully to learn about the old ways of making them. She and Julian tried making their pots in different ways until they had worked out the best way to make beautiful, shiny black pots.

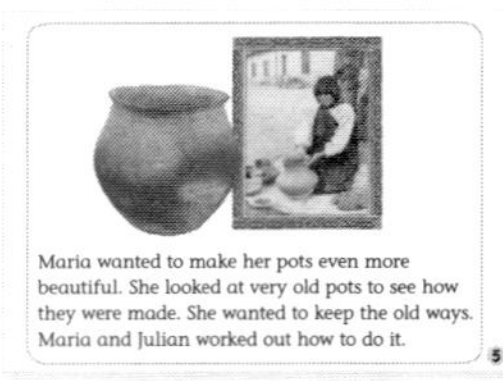
Minibook, page 5

Maria painted and polished her pots to make them shine. Julian painted designs and patterns on them, such as water, snakes, and feathers. People knew that Maria's pots were the finest and very best. Her shiny black pots with black painted designs made her famous. Today, her beautiful art is prized by people and shown in museums.

Minibook, page 6

Maria taught members of her family how to make pottery. She shared the old ways, as well as the new ways she had learned to make the pottery even better. As a mother, a grandmother, and an aunt, she passed down the traditions of her people to the future generations.

Minibook, page 7

Dictionary

Look at the picture. Read the word.
Write the word on the line.

Content Vocabulary

aunt

____

clay

____

clay pots

____

married

____

metal pots

____

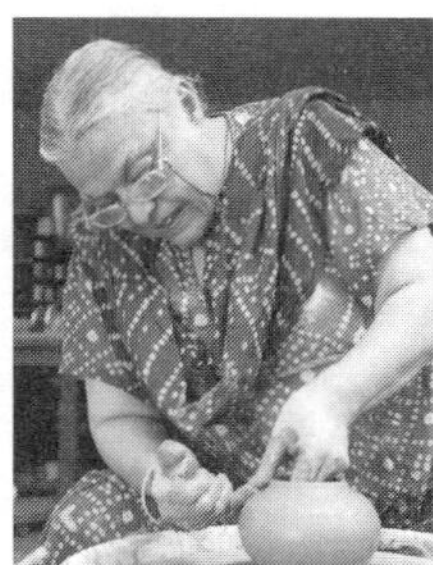

potter

____

pueblo

____

railroad

____

Words to Know

beautiful	bought	brought
learned	liked	painted
shiny	worked	

Maria Martinez
Native American Potter

Name: _______________________________

Maria was born long ago in a little pueblo, or town. She lived in a little house made of adobe.

1

Maria watched her aunt make pots out of clay.
That is how Maria learned to make pots.

2

The railroad came to Maria's pueblo. It brought new things, such as metal pots. It brought new people, too. The people liked Maria's clay pots. They bought the beautiful pots as art.

3

Maria grew up making clay pots. She was a potter. She married Julian and they made pots together. Maria shaped pots from clay, and Julian painted them.

4

Maria wanted to make her pots even more beautiful. She looked at very old pots to see how they were made. She wanted to keep the old ways. Maria and Julian worked out how to do it.

5

Maria's pots were shiny and black. Some had pictures on them. Her pots were the very best. Many people still buy Maria's beautiful art.

6

Maria was a mother, a grandmother, and an aunt. She shared her ways with her family. Maria was a potter who helped other people become potters, too.

7

I Read and Understand

Read and answer.

1. Maria Martinez was _____.

   ○ a painter
   ○ a potter

2. Maria learned by watching _____.

   ○ her aunt
   ○ her grandmother

3. The railroad brought _____.

   ○ potters
   ○ new things

4. Maria wanted to keep _____.

   ○ the old pots
   ○ the old ways

5. Maria's beautiful pots were _____.

   ○ shiny and black
   ○ metal

Name: _______________________________

I Read Closely

Read. Mark the sentence that goes with the picture.

○ Maria was born long
ago in a little pueblo.

○ Maria grew up making
clay pots.

○ Maria shaped the pots,
and Julian painted
them.

○ The people liked
Maria's clay pots.

○ Maria's pots were
shiny and black.

○ Maria watched her
aunt make pots.

○ The railroad brought
new people.

○ She shared her ways
with her family.

Name: _______________________________

Words I Know

Read and answer.

1. A _____ is a town.
   - ○ shiny
   - ○ pueblo
   - ○ potter

2. My _____ is a potter.
   - ○ people
   - ○ past
   - ○ aunt

3. It is a _____ pot.
   - ○ learn
   - ○ clay
   - ○ railroad

4. The new pot is _____.
   - ○ metal
   - ○ married
   - ○ visitor

5. We ride on the _____.
   - ○ past
   - ○ pueblo
   - ○ railroad

   Reading Comprehension: Nonfiction • EMC 3261 • © Evan-Moor Corporation

Name: _______________________

I Can Write

Look at the pictures.
Tell how each one was part of Maria's life.

1. _______________________________

____

____

2. _______________________________

____

____

3. _______________________________

____

____

Biography
George Washington Carver

LEVEL F

Lesson Objective
Students will learn that George Washington Carver used science to learn more about soil and farming.

Content Knowledge
Humans affect the land. Humans can change the land and the soil by planting different crops.

Lesson Preparation

Reproduce and distribute to each student one copy of the dictionary page (p. 105), the minibook pages (pp. 106–109), and the activity pages (pp. 110–113).

Student Minibook: Reproduce the minibook pages. Cut them in half and staple them together in numerical order to make an 8-page booklet.

Learn

1 Build Background

2 Introduce the Vocabulary
Dictionary

3 Read the Texts
George Washington Carver Minibook
Teacher's Complex Text

Analyze

4 Reading Comprehension Activities
I Read and Understand
I Read Closely

5 Close Reading Activity
Oral Discussion Questions

6 Vocabulary Activity
Words I Know

Write

7 Writing Activity
I Can Write

1 Build Background

Explain to students that plants need air, water, sunlight, and nutrients from the soil, or dirt, in order to grow. Nutrients are vitamins or minerals in soil. Plants take in water and nutrients through their roots. Some plants use up the nutrients in the soil, and the land starts to grow fewer plants. Other plants put nutrients back into the soil.

2 Introduce the Vocabulary

Content Vocabulary Point to each pictured word. Read the word aloud and have students echo you. Then have them write the word on the line. Explain any phonetic structures that are unfamiliar to your students. Discuss word meanings as needed. Point out that the word *wagon* can mean "a carriage pulled by a horse" or "a toy that children play with."

Words to Know Point to each word and read it aloud. Have students echo you.

     Reading Comprehension: Nonfiction • EMC 3261 • © Evan-Moor Corporation

3 Read the Texts

Minibook Guide students in reading the minibook together aloud.

Teacher's Complex Text Have students look at the pictures in their minibooks as you read aloud the corresponding Teacher's Complex Text on page 104. Say: *Look at the pictures in your book as I read you more information about the life of the famous scientist, George Washington Carver. Look at the picture on page 1. Listen as I read.*

4 Reading Comprehension Activities

Guide students through completing the activities on pages 110 and 111. Encourage them to look in their minibooks to find information.

5 Close Reading Activity

Oral Discussion Use the Oral Discussion Questions on the right to guide students in a discussion about what they have read and heard. Before you begin, make sure each student has colored pencils and his or her minibook.

Begin by reading aloud a question and having students answer the question and mark the answer in their minibooks.

6 Vocabulary Activity

Guide students through the vocabulary activity on page 112. After they finish, ask them to find and circle the names of two different types of plants. (peanut, cotton)

7 Writing Activity

Guide students through the writing activity on page 113. Have them use information from their minibook and the Teacher's Complex Text. Their sentences should relate to the story. Then have volunteers read aloud their sentences.

Oral Discussion Questions

1. **Who is this book about?** (*George Washington Carver*) **Draw a green line under his name.** (title page)

2. **What did people call George Washington Carver when he was a boy?** (*"The Plant Doctor"*) **Draw an orange line under the sentence that tells why he was given that name.** (*George was a boy who loved plants.*) (page 1)

3. **George Washington Carver studied plant science in college. Whom did he want to help?** (*poor cotton farmers*) **Draw a red line under the answer.** (page 2)

4. **Reread page 3. Use purple to circle the name of the plant that wore out the soil. Use brown to circle the name of the plant that helped the soil.** (*purple—cotton; brown—peanut*) (page 3)

5. **Why did George Washington Carver use a special wagon?** (*Instead of asking farmers to come to school, he took the school to the farmers.*) **Write *school* next to the wagon on page 4.**

6. **If farmers grew peanuts, they would have to sell them. How did George Washington Carver help farmers sell their peanuts?** (*He made hundreds of new things from peanuts.*) **Where did George work on this problem?** (*in his science lab*) **Draw a red X on the page that shows the answer.** (page 6)

7. **Name two ways George Washington Carver helped farmers.** (*He taught them about peanut plants that helped the soil. He found hundreds of new ways in which people could use peanuts.*)

George Washington Carver

George Washington Carver was born an enslaved person in 1864, during the War Between the States. When President Lincoln freed enslaved people, it meant that George was freed, too. Growing up, George loved plants. He had his own secret garden and people would bring him their sick plants to get his advice. Young George was known as "The Plant Doctor."

Minibook, page 1

Many people who had been freed became cotton farmers. Others, like George Washington Carver, were able to go to school for the first time. He went to college, where he studied art and music. George's teacher saw that he was good with plants and thought he should study plant science. George knew that many cotton farmers were poor. He thought he could help them if he learned more about plants.

Minibook, page 2

George Washington Carver saw that growing cotton every year wore out the soil. It took out the nutrients that plants need in order to grow. So George looked for other plants that could put those nutrients back into the soil. He found that peanuts, sweet potatoes, and black-eyed peas helped put back what years of growing cotton had taken away from the soil.

Minibook, page 3

George Washington Carver knew that farmers could not leave their farms to go to school. So he had a special wagon made. He named it the Jesup Agricultural Wagon, after the man who gave money to build it. The Jesup Wagon was like a moving classroom. Carver used it to show farmers plants that build up the soil, as well as how to grow them.

Minibook, page 4

George Washington Carver showed farmers how to build up the soil by planting peanut plants one year and cotton plants the next. But the farmers didn't know what to do with all the peanuts. They needed to sell them, but people didn't use a lot of peanuts. At that time, peanuts were only used as food for pigs.

Minibook, page 5

George Washington Carver went back to his science lab. He took apart the peanut plants. He worked to make useful products. He knew that if people would buy peanut products, then farmers would plant more peanuts. The peanuts would add nutrients to the soil and other plants would grow better. Carver invented hundreds of new things from peanuts, including peanut oil, medicines, plastics, fuels, paints, dyes, makeup, and food recipes.

Minibook, page 6

George Washington Carver helped farmers grow better crops. He showed them that peanuts would help the soil. He invented many new uses for peanuts so that farmers could sell the peanuts they grew. He used science to help others.

Minibook, page 7

Name: _______________________

Dictionary

Look at the picture. Read the word.
Write the word on the line.

Content Vocabulary

cotton

____

doctor

____

farmer

____

lab

____

peanuts

____

plant

____

soil

____

wagon

____

Words to Know

better	college	hundreds
school	science	sell

George Washington Carver

Name: _______________________

George was a boy who loved plants.
People called him "The Plant Doctor."

1

He studied plant science at college.
He wanted to help poor cotton farmers.

2

Cotton plants wore out the soil.
He found that peanut plants helped the soil.

3

George made a school on a special wagon.
He went to farms. He showed farmers how
to make the soil good again.

4

George taught farmers to grow peanuts.
But people did not use peanuts.
The farmers could not sell them.

5

George went back to his science lab.
He made hundreds of new things from peanuts.

6

George helped farmers grow better crops
and sell them. He used science to help others.

7

I Read and Understand

Read and answer.

1. George helped others .
   - with college
   - with science

2. Cotton plants .
   - helped the soil
   - wore out the soil

3. Peanut plants .
   - helped the soil
   - wore out the soil

4. George found hundreds of _____.
   - ways to use cotton
   - ways to use peanuts

5. Did the wagon take the school to the farmers?
   - yes
   - no

Name: _______________________________

I Read Closely

Read. Mark the sentence that goes with the picture.

○ George made hundreds of things from peanuts.

○ People called George "The Plant Doctor."

○ George went back to his science lab.

○ George made a school on a special wagon.

○ George used science to help others.

○ George studied plant science at college.

○ George taught farmers to grow peanuts.

○ George was a boy who loved plants.

Words I Know

Read and answer.

1. Plant it in the ____.
   - ○ peanut
   - ○ soil
   - ○ science

2. The farmer grows ____.
   - ○ cotton
   - ○ school
   - ○ hundreds

3. He has peanuts to ____.
   - ○ lab
   - ○ sell
   - ○ soil

4. She wants to be a ____.
   - ○ wagon
   - ○ better
   - ○ doctor

5. Plant science helps ____.
   - ○ college
   - ○ farmers
   - ○ wagon

Name: _______________________________

I Can Write

Tell about the life of George Washington Carver.
Write a sentence for each picture.

1. _______________________________

____

____

2. _______________________________

____

____

3. _______________________________

____

____

How-to

How to Make the President's Breakfast

Lesson Objective Students will learn about what the first president of the United States liked to eat for breakfast and how his favorite breakfast food was made.

Content Knowledge The United States has had many presidents who lived in different time periods and followed different customs.

Lesson Preparation

Reproduce and distribute to each student one copy of the dictionary page (p. 117), the student text (p. 118), and the activity pages (pp. 119–123).

Learn

1 Build Background

2 Introduce the Vocabulary
Dictionary

3 Read the Texts
How to Make the President's Breakfast
   Student Text
Teacher's Complex Text

Analyze

4 Reading Comprehension Activities
I Read and Understand
I Read Closely

5 Close Reading Activity
Oral Discussion Questions

6 Vocabulary Activity
Words I Know

Write

7 Writing Activities
I Can Write
What I Learned

1 Build Background

Explain to students that George Washington was one of the founders of the United States of America. He helped to set up the government of the new country. He was also the first president, and he is known as the "father of our country." The capital of the United States, Washington, D.C., is named in honor of him.

2 Introduce the Vocabulary

Content Vocabulary Point to each pictured word. Read the word aloud and have students echo you. Then have them write the word on the line. Explain any phonetic structures that are unfamiliar to your students. Discuss word meanings as needed.

Words to Know Point to each word and read it aloud. Have students echo you. Point out that the word *swimming* can mean "moving through water using arms and legs" or "covered in liquid."

3 Read the Texts

Student Text Guide students in reading the text together aloud.

Teacher's Complex Text Have students look at their text page and listen as you read aloud the corresponding Teacher's Complex Text on page 116. Say: *Listen as I read you more information about President George Washington's favorite breakfast.* Have students follow along as you read the recipe at the end of the text.

4 Reading Comprehension Activities

Guide students through completing the activities on pages 119 and 120. Encourage them to look in their text to find information.

5 Close Reading Activity

Oral Discussion Use the Oral Discussion Questions on the right to guide students in a discussion about what they have read and heard. Before you begin, make sure each student has colored pencils and his or her text.

Begin by reading aloud a question and having students answer the question and mark the answer in their text.

6 Vocabulary Activity

Guide students through the vocabulary activity on page 121. After they finish, ask them to find three compound words on the page and draw a blue line under each one.

7 Writing Activities

Guide students through the *I Can Write* activity. Have them use information from their text and the Teacher's Complex Text. For the *What I Learned* activity, have them refer to their text in order to complete the list of ingredients.

Oral Discussion Questions

1. **What did George Washington like to eat for breakfast?** (*He ate hoecakes for breakfast.*) **Make a blue dot beside the sentence that tells the answer.**

2. **How did he eat them? Did he eat them plain?** (*No; the president liked them swimming in butter and honey.*) **Draw an orange line under the answer.**

3. **Do hoecakes remind you of something else?** (*Hoecakes are like pancakes.*) **Make a brown dot next to the answer. How are they alike or different?** (*E.g., They are little cakes made by cooking the batter in a pan. You eat them for breakfast. They are different because they are made with cornmeal.*) **What else could you put on warm hoecakes before eating them?** (*E.g., blueberries, nuts*)

4. **What can you learn to do by reading this text?** (*You can learn how to make hoecakes.*)

5. **Why do you think the author chose to write a recipe for hoecakes?** (*E.g., because George Washington ate them for breakfast; to teach something about the past*)

6. **Find the title of the recipe and circle it with green.** (*Hoecakes*) **How would the text have changed if George Washington had eaten oatmeal for breakfast?** (*There would probably be a recipe for oatmeal.*) **What would the new recipe title be?** (*Oatmeal*)

7. **What was the author's purpose in writing this text?** (*to give information about George Washington and to explain how to make hoecakes*)

How to Make the President's Breakfast

George Washington was the first president of the United States of America. Have you ever wondered what he was like as a person? For example, what did an important man like President Washington eat for breakfast? Well, it is said that Washington got out of bed before the sun was up. He wrote or read until 7 o'clock in summer, 7:30 in winter. Then he ate a breakfast of three small hoecakes. Hoecakes are simple pancakes made of cornmeal. He liked them swimming in butter and honey. He washed them down with three cups of tea, no cream.

How did hoecakes get their name? We can't be sure. Some people believe that once upon a time hoecakes were cooked on a garden hoe over the fire! Pancakes are cooked in a pan; hoecakes were cooked on a hoe. But other people think a hoe was really another name for a type of griddle. Either way, here is a very old recipe that makes the same kind of hoecakes George Washington liked to eat for breakfast. Remember one very important rule: **Always have an adult help you cook.**

Hoecakes

You need:

8¾ cups white cornmeal
1¼ teaspoons dry yeast
warm water
1 egg
cooking oil
honey and butter

1. Mix 4 cups of cornmeal and the yeast in a bowl.
2. Add enough warm water so it is like pancake batter.
3. Cover the batter and set it in a warm place overnight.
4. In the morning, stir in the rest of the cornmeal.
5. Add the egg and enough warm water so it is like pancake batter again.
6. Cover for 15 minutes.
7. To cook the batter, add cooking oil to a pan. Heat it up.
8. Pour the batter into the pan with a large spoon.
9. After the hoecakes are brown on one side, turn them over. Let them brown on the other side.
10. Eat the hoecakes warm, with butter and honey.

Name: _______________________________

Dictionary

Look at the picture. Read the word.
Write the word on the line.

Content Vocabulary

batter

butter

cornmeal

hoe

hoecakes

honey

teaspoon

yeast

Words to Know

| cook | heat | morning | oil |
| overnight | president | swimming | warm |

How to Make the President's Breakfast

George Washington was our first president. Not many people know that he ate hoecakes for breakfast. Hoecakes are like pancakes. The president liked them swimming in butter and honey.

Why are they called hoecakes? Maybe because they were cooked on a garden hoe! No one knows for sure. You can eat hoecakes cooked in a pan. **Always have an adult help you cook.**

Hoecakes

You need:

8¾ cups white cornmeal
1¼ teaspoons dry yeast
warm water
1 egg
cooking oil
honey and butter

1. Mix 4 cups of cornmeal and the yeast in a bowl.
2. Add enough warm water so it is like pancake batter.
3. Cover the batter and set it in a warm place overnight.
4. In the morning, stir in the rest of the cornmeal.
5. Add the egg and more warm water.
6. Cover for 15 minutes.
7. To cook the batter, add cooking oil to a pan. Heat it up.
8. Pour the batter into the pan with a large spoon.
9. After the hoecakes are brown on one side, turn them over. Let them brown on the other side.
10. Eat the hoecakes warm, with butter and honey.

Name: _______________________

I Read and Understand

Read and answer.

1. George Washington liked _____.

   ○ eggs
   ○ hoecakes

2. Hoecakes are made from _____.

   ○ pancakes
   ○ cornmeal

3. Let the batter set _____.

   ○ all day
   ○ overnight

4. In the morning, _____.

   ○ go swimming
   ○ add the egg

5. Eat them with _____.

   ○ butter and honey
   ○ the president

Name: _______________________________

I Read Closely

Look at the picture. Answer the question.

How to Make Hoecakes

1. What is the first thing to do?

____

____

2. How do you cook the batter?

____

____

3. How do you eat the hoecakes?

____

____

Name: ________________________________

Words I Know

Read and answer.

1. Please have another ____.
   - ○ butter
   - ○ cook
   - ○ hoecake

2. Mix some ____ and cornmeal.
   - ○ yeast
   - ○ morning
   - ○ swimming

3. The hoecakes are ____.
   - ○ honey
   - ○ warm
   - ○ night

4. Do you like ____ on hoecakes?
   - ○ butter
   - ○ hoe
   - ○ president

5. George Washington was our first ____.
   - ○ morning
   - ○ teaspoon
   - ○ president

Name: ______________________________

I Can Write

Write the words to finish the sentence.

Word Box

with butter and honey   into the pan

after they are brown   heat it up

1. Add cooking oil to the pan and ________________________.

2. Pour the batter ________________________.

3. Turn the hoecakes over ________________________.

4. Eat them warm, ________________________.

Write a sentence that tells how hoecakes may have gotten
their name.

____

____

What I Learned

Tell what you need to cook hoecakes.
Write the missing things.

How to Make Hoecakes

8¾ cups ________________________

1¼ teaspoons ________________________

warm ________________________

1 ________________________

cooking ________________________

honey and ________________________

Draw a picture that shows all the things on the list.

Answer Key

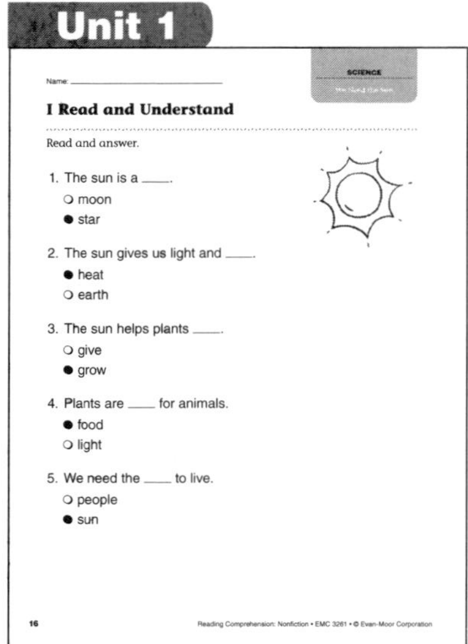

Page 16

Page 17

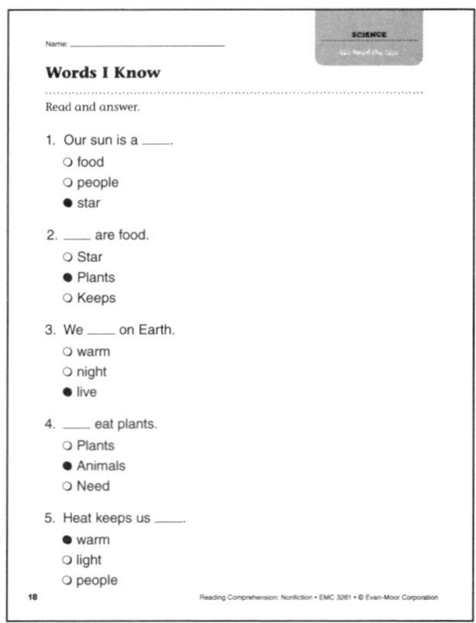

Page 18

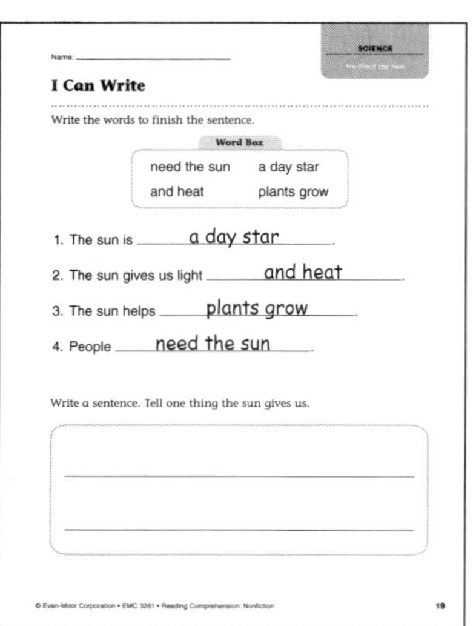

Page 19

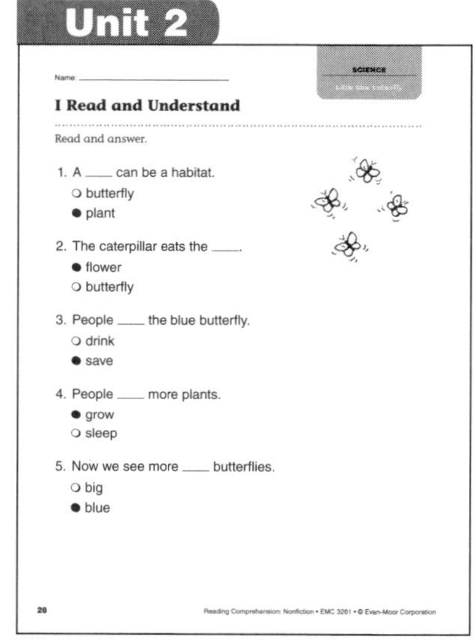

Page 28

Page 29

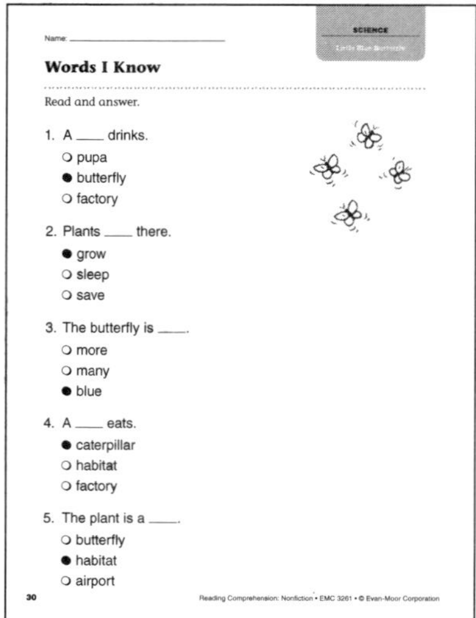

Page 30

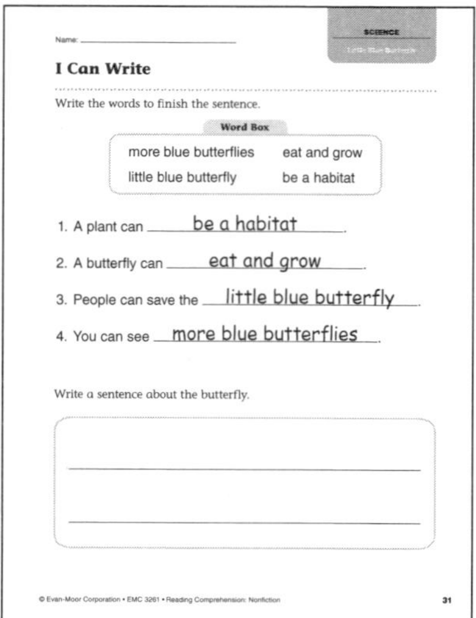

Page 31

124

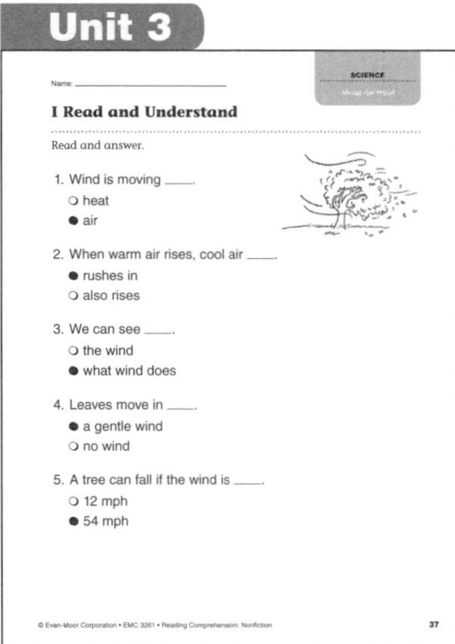

Page 37

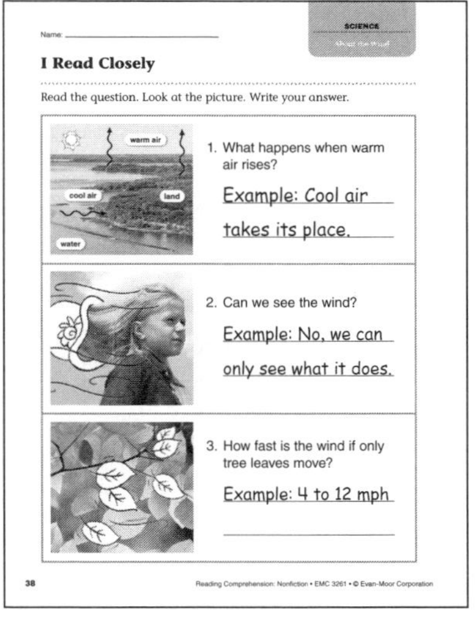

Page 38

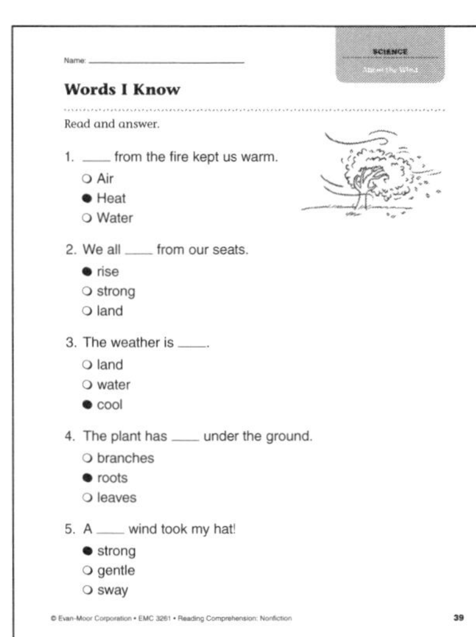

Page 39

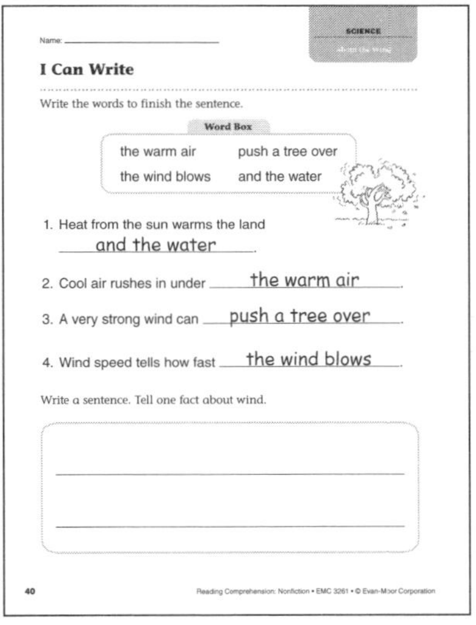

Page 40

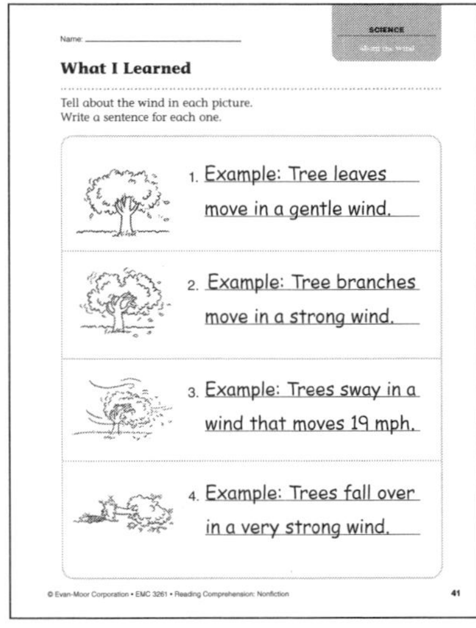

Page 41

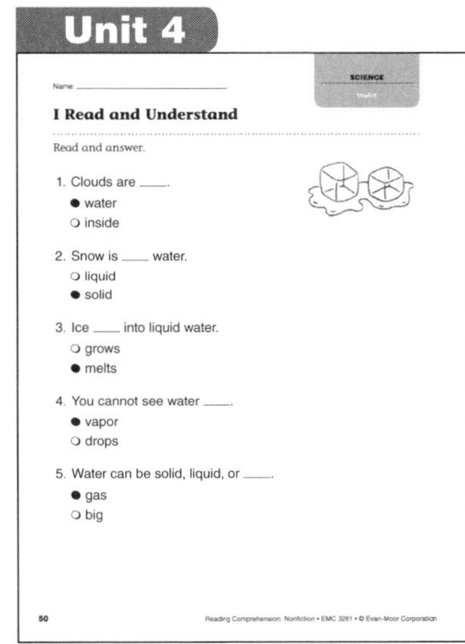

Page 50

Page 51

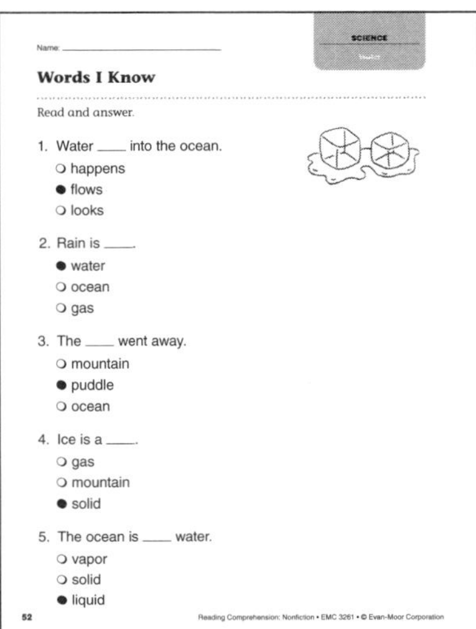

Page 52

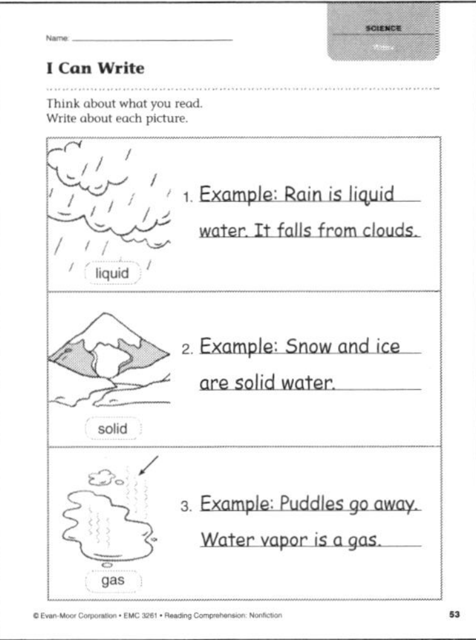

Page 53

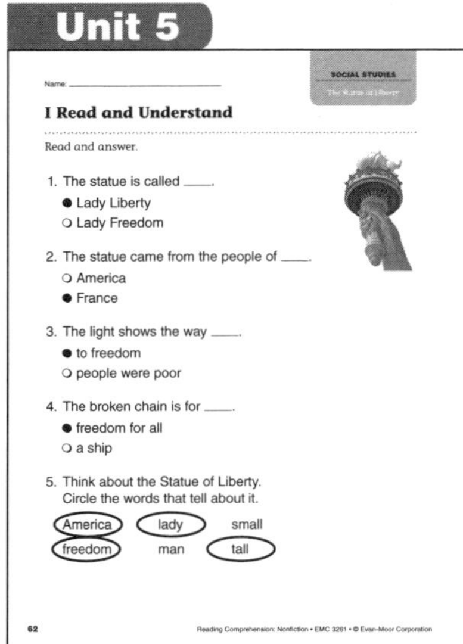

Page 62

Page 63

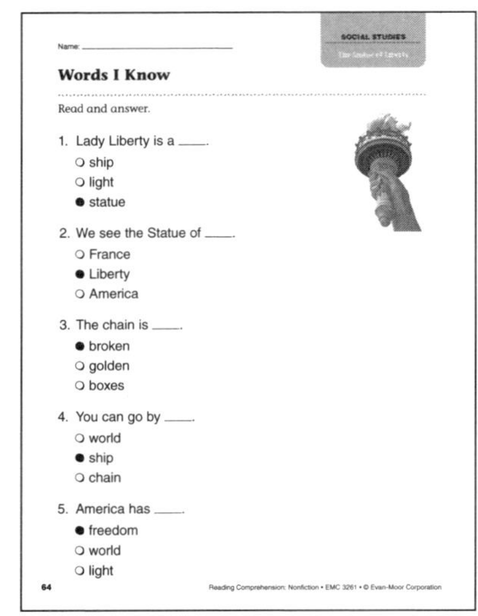

Page 64

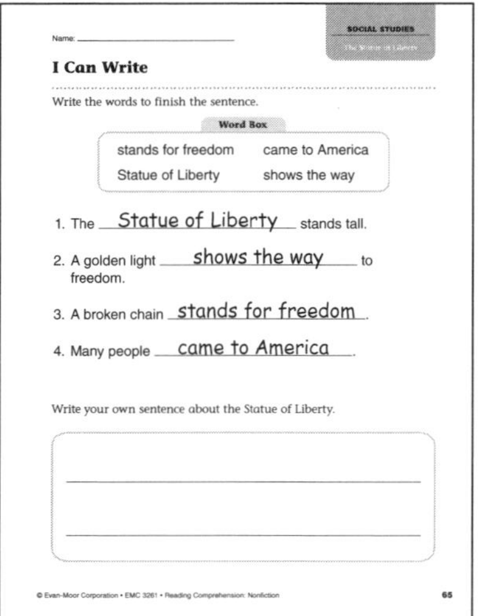

Page 65

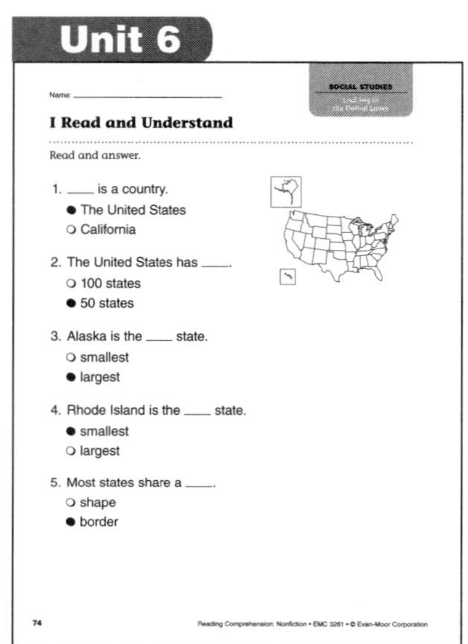

Page 74

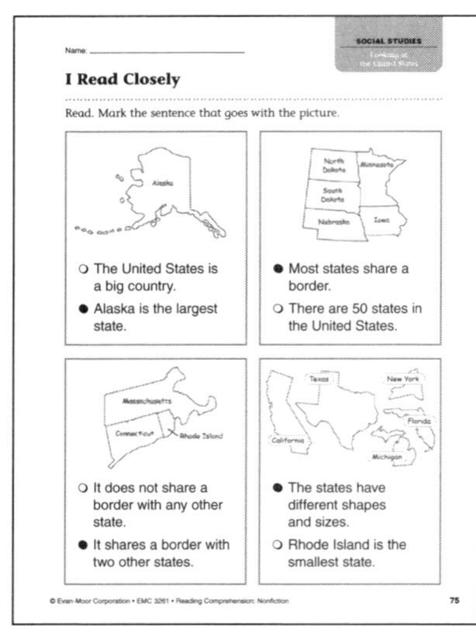

Page 75

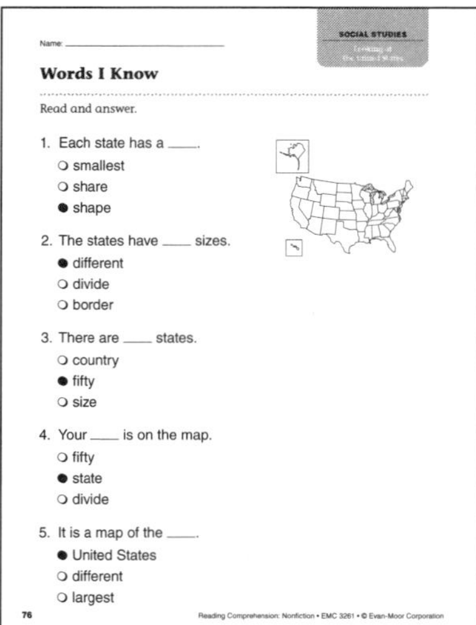

Page 76

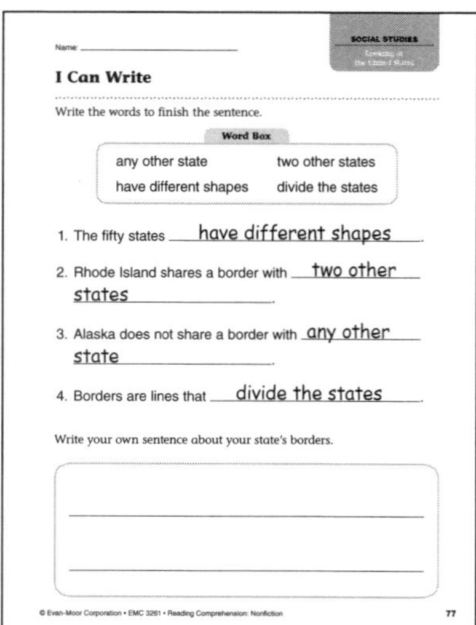

Page 77

126

Page 86

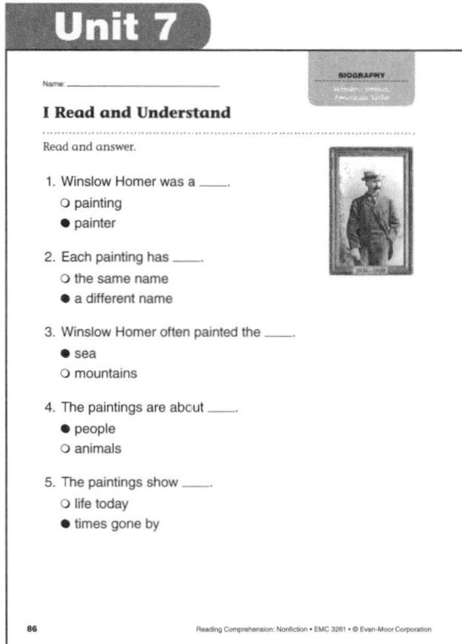

Name: _______________

I Read and Understand

Read and answer.

1. Winslow Homer was a _____
   ○ painting
   ● painter

2. Each painting has _____
   ○ the same name
   ● a different name

3. Winslow Homer often painted the _____
   ● sea
   ○ mountains

4. The paintings are about _____
   ● people
   ○ animals

5. The paintings show _____
   ○ life today
   ● times gone by

Page 87

Name: _______________

I Read Closely

Read. Mark the sentence that goes with the picture.

● The Country School
○ The New Novel

○ Girl with Hay Rake
● The New Novel

● Breezing Up
○ Snap the Whip

○ The Country School
● Waiting for Dad

Page 88

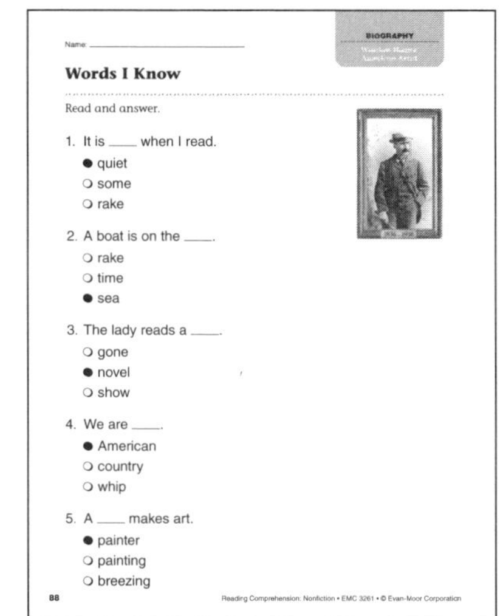

Name: _______________

Words I Know

Read and answer.

1. It is _____ when I read.
   ● quiet
   ○ some
   ○ rake

2. A boat is on the _____
   ○ rake
   ○ time
   ● sea

3. The lady reads a _____
   ○ gone
   ● novel
   ○ show

4. We are _____
   ● American
   ○ country
   ○ whip

5. A _____ makes art.
   ● painter
   ○ painting
   ○ breezing

Page 89

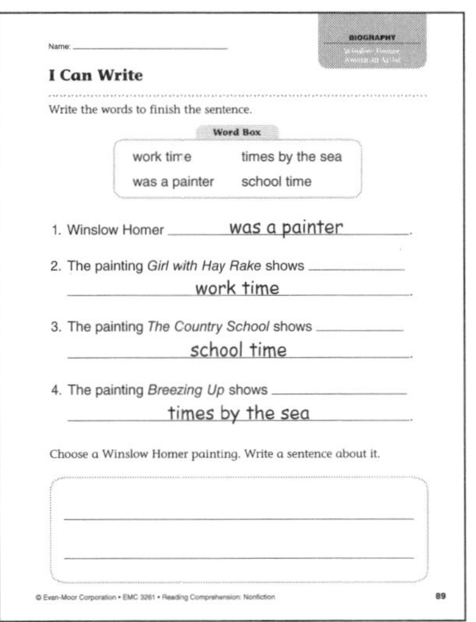

Name: _______________

I Can Write

Write the words to finish the sentence.

Word Box

work time   times by the sea
was a painter   school time

1. Winslow Homer _____ was a painter

2. The painting *Girl with Hay Rake* shows _____ work time

3. The painting *The Country School* shows _____ school time

4. The painting *Breezing Up* shows _____ times by the sea

Choose a Winslow Homer painting. Write a sentence about it.

Page 98

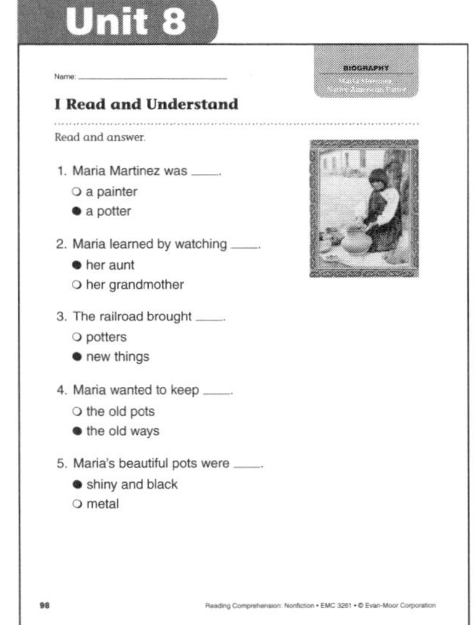

Name: _______________

I Read and Understand

Read and answer.

1. Maria Martinez was _____
   ○ a painter
   ● a potter

2. Maria learned by watching _____
   ● her aunt
   ○ her grandmother

3. The railroad brought _____
   ○ potters
   ● new things

4. Maria wanted to keep _____
   ○ the old pots
   ● the old ways

5. Maria's beautiful pots were _____
   ● shiny and black
   ○ metal

Page 99

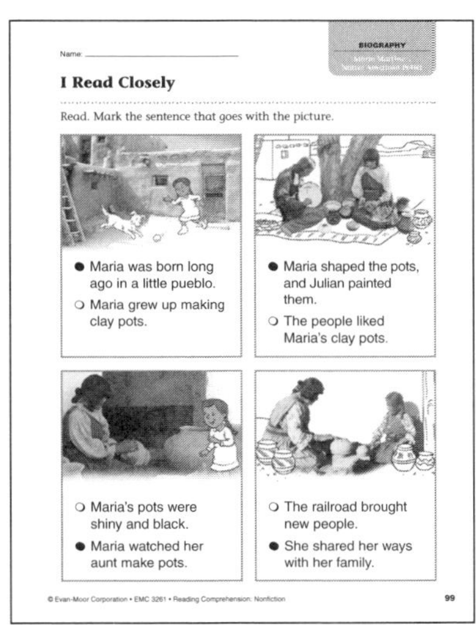

Name: _______________

I Read Closely

Read. Mark the sentence that goes with the picture.

● Maria was born long ago in a little pueblo.
○ Maria grew up making clay pots.

● Maria shaped the pots, and Julian painted them.
○ The people liked Maria's clay pots.

○ Maria's pots were shiny and black.
● Maria watched her aunt make pots.

○ The railroad brought new people.
● She shared her ways with her family.

Page 100

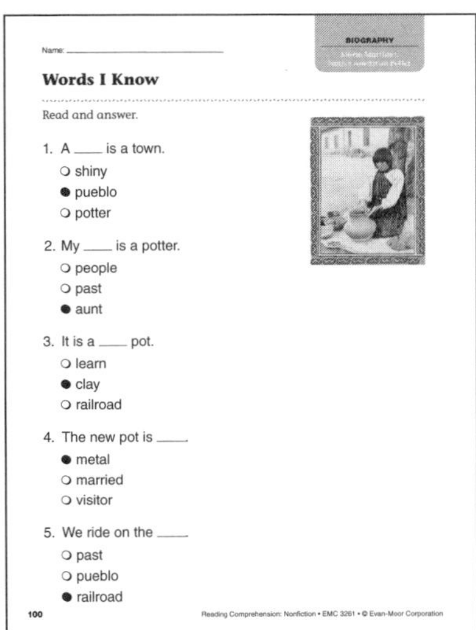

Name: _______________

Words I Know

Read and answer.

1. A _____ is a town.
   ○ shiny
   ● pueblo
   ○ potter

2. My _____ is a potter.
   ○ people
   ○ past
   ● aunt

3. It is a _____ pot.
   ○ learn
   ● clay
   ○ railroad

4. The new pot is _____
   ● metal
   ○ married
   ○ visitor

5. We ride on the _____
   ○ past
   ○ pueblo
   ● railroad

Page 101

Name: _______________

I Can Write

Look at the pictures.
Tell how each one was part of Maria's life.

1. Example: Maria was born in a pueblo in New Mexico.

   pueblo

2. Example: The railroad brought visitors who wanted beautiful pots.

   railroad

3. Example: Maria Martinez made beautiful, shiny black pots.

   pot

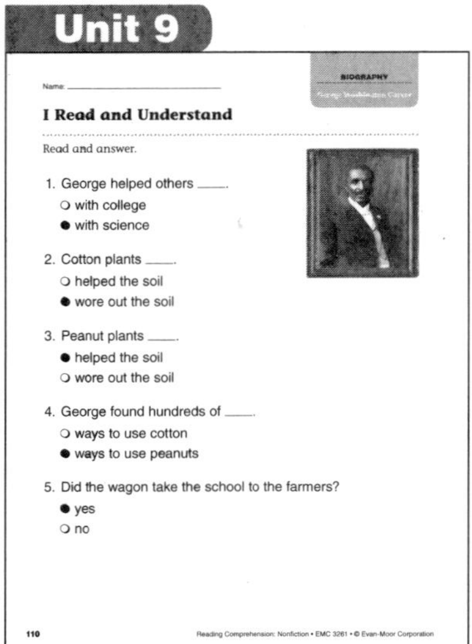

I Read and Understand

Read and answer.

1. George helped others ____.
   ○ with college
   ● with science

2. Cotton plants ____.
   ○ helped the soil
   ● wore out the soil

3. Peanut plants ____.
   ● helped the soil
   ○ wore out the soil

4. George found hundreds of ____.
   ○ ways to use cotton
   ● ways to use peanuts

5. Did the wagon take the school to the farmers?
   ● yes
   ○ no

Page 110

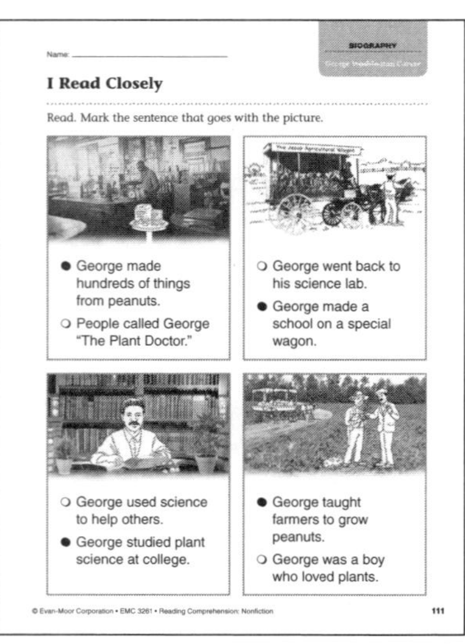

I Read Closely

Read. Mark the sentence that goes with the picture.

● George made hundreds of things from peanuts.
○ People called George "The Plant Doctor."

○ George went back to his science lab.
● George made a school on a special wagon.

○ George used science to help others.
● George studied plant science at college.

○ George taught farmers to grow peanuts.
● George was a boy who loved plants.

Page 111

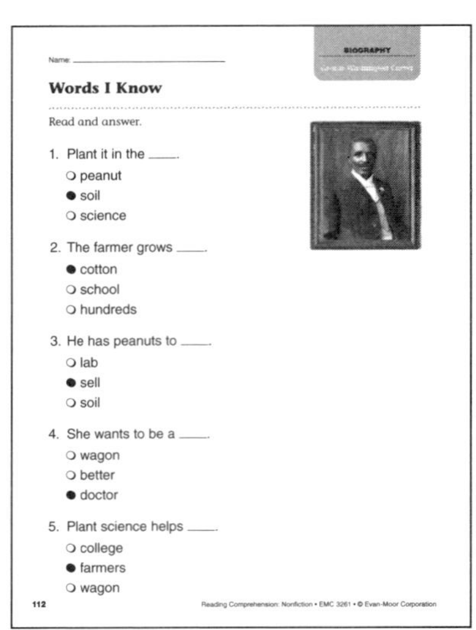

Words I Know

Read and answer.

1. Plant it in the ____.
   ○ peanut
   ● soil
   ○ science

2. The farmer grows ____.
   ● cotton
   ○ school
   ○ hundreds

3. He has peanuts to ____.
   ○ lab
   ● sell
   ○ soil

4. She wants to be a ____.
   ○ wagon
   ○ better
   ● doctor

5. Plant science helps ____.
   ○ college
   ● farmers
   ○ wagon

Page 112

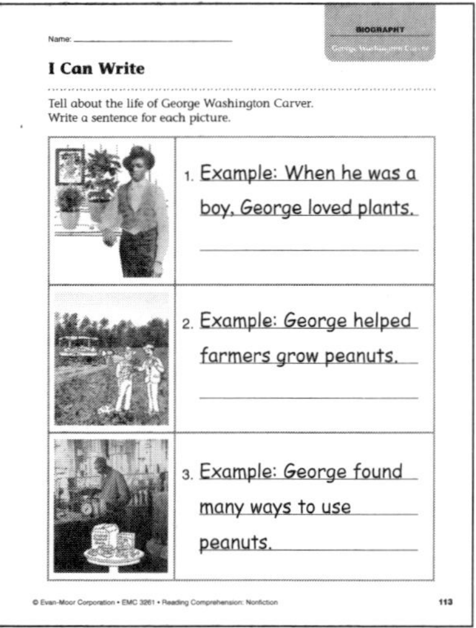

I Can Write

Tell about the life of George Washington Carver. Write a sentence for each picture.

1. Example: When he was a boy, George loved plants.

2. Example: George helped farmers grow peanuts.

3. Example: George found many ways to use peanuts.

Page 113

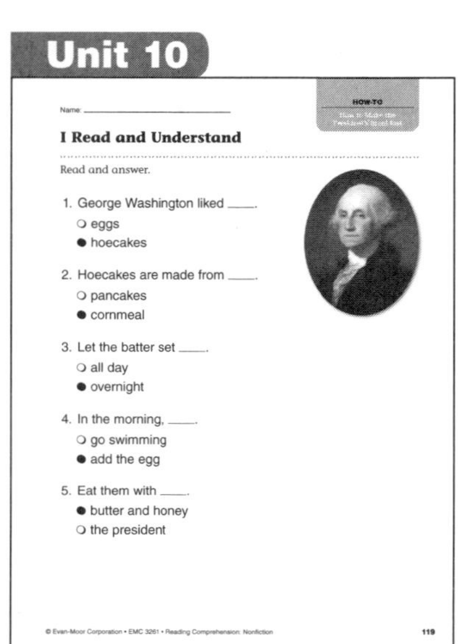

I Read and Understand

Read and answer.

1. George Washington liked ____.
   ○ eggs
   ● hoecakes

2. Hoecakes are made from ____.
   ○ pancakes
   ● cornmeal

3. Let the batter set ____.
   ○ all day
   ● overnight

4. In the morning, ____.
   ○ go swimming
   ● add the egg

5. Eat them with ____.
   ● butter and honey
   ○ the president

Page 119

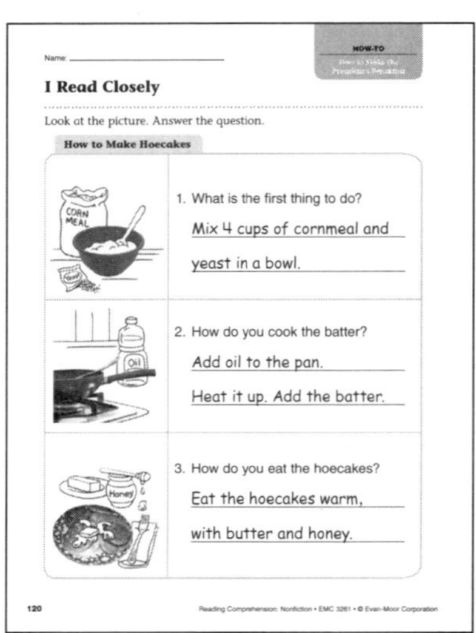

I Read Closely

Look at the picture. Answer the question.

How to Make Hoecakes

1. What is the first thing to do?
   Mix 4 cups of cornmeal and yeast in a bowl.

2. How do you cook the batter?
   Add oil to the pan. Heat it up. Add the batter.

3. How do you eat the hoecakes?
   Eat the hoecakes warm, with butter and honey.

Page 120

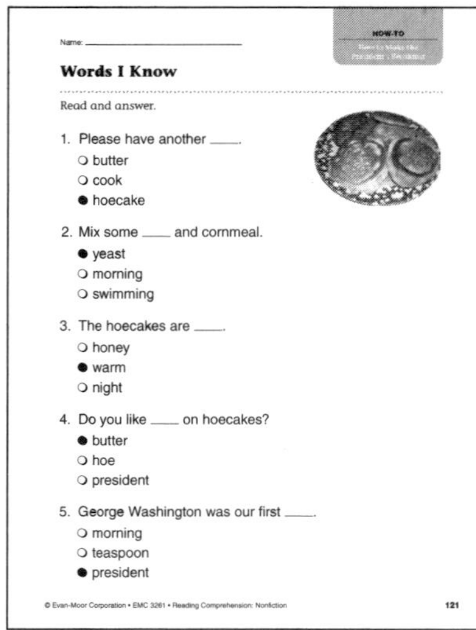

Words I Know

Read and answer.

1. Please have another ____.
   ○ butter
   ○ cook
   ● hoecake

2. Mix some ____ and cornmeal.
   ● yeast
   ○ morning
   ○ swimming

3. The hoecakes are ____.
   ○ honey
   ● warm
   ○ night

4. Do you like ____ on hoecakes?
   ● butter
   ○ hoe
   ○ president

5. George Washington was our first ____.
   ○ morning
   ○ teaspoon
   ● president

Page 121

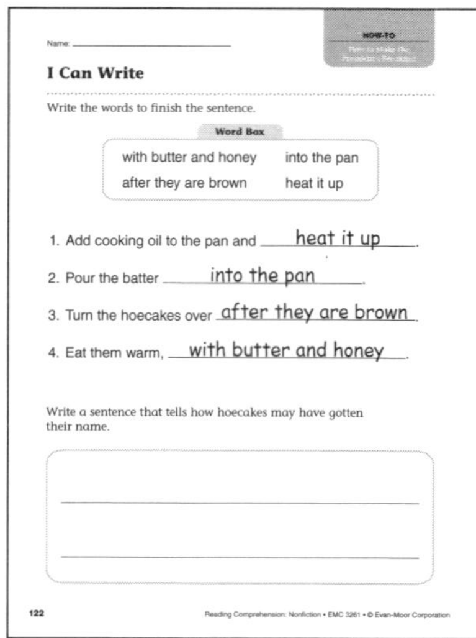

I Can Write

Write the words to finish the sentence.

Word Box

with butter and honey	into the pan
after they are brown	heat it up

1. Add cooking oil to the pan and ___ heat it up

2. Pour the batter ___ into the pan

3. Turn the hoecakes over ___ after they are brown

4. Eat them warm, ___ with butter and honey

Write a sentence that tells how hoecakes may have gotten their name.

Page 122

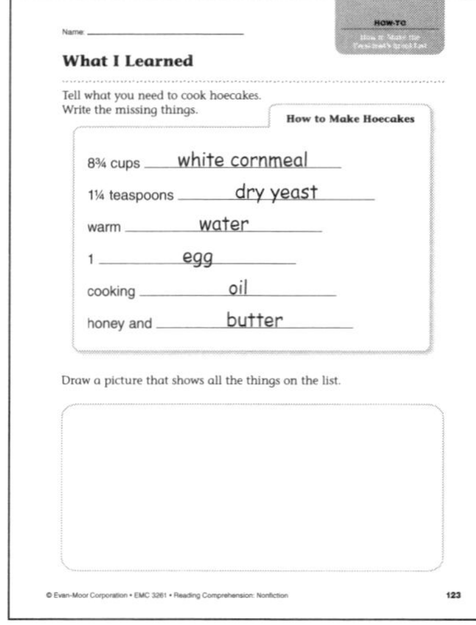

What I Learned

Tell what you need to cook hoecakes. Write the missing things.

How to Make Hoecakes

8¾ cups	white cornmeal
1¼ teaspoons	dry yeast
warm	water
1	egg
cooking	oil
honey and	butter

Draw a picture that shows all the things on the list.

Page 123

128